SURVIVORS: Women of the Southwest

RITA KASCH CHEGIN

Yucca Tree Press

First Printing   1991

Cover design by Marva McGee.

Library of Congress Cataloging in Publication Data.

Chegin, Rita Kasch

SURVIVORS: Women of the Southwest

1. Southwest United States - History.
2. New Mexico - History.
3. Women - History. 4. Oral Histories.
I. Rita Kasch Chegin. II. Title

Library of Congress Catalog Card Number: 91-066179

ISBN 0-9622940-4-7

*This book is lovingly dedicated to
John J., Teresa, Cathy, and John Robert.*

Acknowledgments

A very special thanks to those who helped *Survivors* become a reality. I truly appreciated the encouragement and interest of the women and their families whose stories are in the book— —all of the women interviewees and J.R. Barton, Aurora and Doyle Banks, Jack Durio, Bill Chilton, G.L. Guthrie, Lester and Eleanor Heinzman, Kathleen Johnson, and Paul Roach, Jr.

For their help with research and technical assistance, I would like to thank— —Linda Blazer, Tim Blevins, Patricia McCann, and Kyla Ogle - Rio Grande Historical Collections; Cheryl Wilson - Special Collections New Mexico State University Library; Ward Redshaw, Virgil Collins, and Don R. Martin for help with photographs; Liz Amezquita, Gloria Hayner Shelly Campbell, Augustina Campos, Lou Damato, Amelia Garcia, Dr. Ben H. Haines, Genevieve Hammond, Alice L. Helfrich, Pat McClernon, Larkin Salazar, Rev. Dennis Tejada, Charles and Claude Tharp, Sophie R. Waldrip, Ron White, and Patsy Yates.

Dr. Joan Jensen, Professor of History, Director of the New Mexico State University Women's Center, and author. For her class, "Born Female," I completed my first oral history. I am so grateful to her for inspiring me to continue doing what is so enjoyable and fulfilling, and I hope interesting reading.

This book was partially funded by the Southwestern New Mexico Area Agency on Aging. We are especially grateful to Mr. Art Bardwell, Director, and the Board of Directors for the SWNM Area Agency on Aging who helped make our project a reality.

Gracias to each one of you.

Photographs were provided by the families unless otherwise noted. Sketch on page 142 by Marva McGee.

Our history books are filled with pages across which men stride bravely, boldly and determined. The characters in these myths are our heroes who crossed the rivers, climbed the mountains, battled the elements and the enemies of man to create our civilized world.

With few exceptions, the roles of the women and children have been ignored. And if not ignored, given only casual mention. Western writers, especially, cast most of their women characters as the little women keeping the home fires burning or the loose ones that surely must have populated every saloon in the West. And it wasn't too long ago when many women writers concocted male pseudonyms in hopes their manuscripts would be more favorably considered by the male editors who headed most publishing houses—and still do.

But all of this is changing now. Social scientists, especially newer historians, are questioning the virtues attributed to some of our heroes and are looking much more closely at the roles women have played in civilization. Research is sometimes difficult because their names do not appear on records and their contributions have been so underestimated. A few of those who were taught reading, writing and arithmetic kept diaries, and a few of these have been preserved so future generations can know what their lives were really like. These books and other memoirs form an intriguing body of literature.

Another important body of literature are the transcripts of oral histories, a rather recent development spurred on by the popular use of tape recorders. This has made it easy to record the thoughts of people, including their memories.

The degree of success of this literature depends, it seems to me, on the compatibility of the interviewer and the interviewee and on the development of a line of questioning. Then, of course, there is the editing.

It always has been said that every person can write one book—the story of his or her life. But most people do not try.

A blank piece of paper can be a scary thing. This is why oral histories are so important. Those who have lived these experiences can bring a more proper perspective to the myths that are our history. These are slices of life not otherwise available, as told by those who were there.

It is too late for many. It is very late for some others. We need to know. We must hurry!

Barbara Funkhauser
Las Cruces, New Mexico
July 1991

It was a privilege to interview the ladies whose stories are in this book. For sharing their memories with me, and now with you, I sincerely thank them.

When I began doing oral interviews in 1979, I wasn't looking for "lost heroines," famous figures in public life, women's rights activists, actresses or artists. I was looking for women from different cultures and backgrounds who could tell me what their lives were really like before and after the turn of the century.

These women talked about what they remembered about their mothers, grandmothers, sometimes great-grandmothers, sisters and other family members. They told me things that even their children didn't know. In their unassuming and honest way, they have passed on important historical information that will never be found in history books. Their reminiscing has revealed the important role women have played in the development of the Southwest.

The review of their lives has shown how women coped from the time of Geronimo and Pancho Villa through wars, depressions, floods, sandstorms, and personal tragedies. The demands of society, discrimination and other problems of every day living during those early years required endurance, courage, loyalty and considerable optimism. I hope I have caught the spirit of these pioneers and you too can recognize the worth of their roles and the importance of their efforts and contributions.

It is important that we realize these women leave as a legacy a gift of stories about the past that no one else can give. It is imperative that we interview elderly men and women before their voices are quiet forever. It is hoped that these true stories will make younger family members realize the importance of getting the remembrances of their elderly relatives and friends on tape. The process of looking inward and looking backward over time at the life one has lived is a natural and healthful integrative process of aging.

Centuries ago "the minstrel sang or chanted each evening in the great hall before young and old, servant and master, the deeds of those who had lived before." The epic song served as a kind of ritual to pass on the dreams and sorrows of a culture from one generation to the next. The elderly need to be asked to look inward and backward over time, to sing their song so that generations to come may know about their dreams and sorrows, their hardships and their happy times.

A line from the Prologue of Elizabeth Barrett Browning's poem, "Curse for a Nation," describes what women have told us in their stories.

"...is very salt, and bitter and good."

Rita Kasch Chegin
Las Cruces, New Mexico
July 1991

~~~~~~
~~~~~~

Table of Contents

SURVIVORS

Icy Carnes and Calvin Banks

$\mathcal{L}$IVIN' THROUGH IT

Icy Carnes Banks

Icy Carnes Banks and her husband, Calvin, were living in a nursing home when I first met them in 1980. Calvin had suffered a stroke, was confined to a wheelchair, and could not speak. Although Icy was in reasonably good health despite her age, the facility administrators allowed her to stay there. Calvin occupied a room with another male patient in the men's wing and Icy shared her room with a woman patient in the women's wing.

Icy was always by her husband's side to help in any way she could. It was an unusual arrangement, but Icy was an unusual woman and it was evident that the years had not weakened her power of persuasion.

Unlike some of the women I interviewed, Icy was anxious to tell the world about her life from early childhood through her eighty-four years.

We lived in a small house on the edge of the Sam Houston National Forest, about forty miles to the north of Houston, Texas. I was born there on March 24, 1896, and spent all of my childhood and most of my adult years in the sawmill area. I was the third child in a family of seven girls and seven boys.

Icy's youth depicts the teamwork necessary to a large family's survival in rural Texas. The Carnes family probably could have "made it" anywhere because they had the secret.

By 1900 some of the land had been cleared for farming, but to support our large family my father, Barney, also worked for the Foster Lumber Company. My mother, Effie, took care of the farming and a large garden that provided food for our family. My father used to call my mother, "old woman." "Old woman, you're the best rustler, but I'm the best manager," he would say affectionately. We raised sugar cane, corn, oats, sweet potatoes, black-eyed peas, purple hump peas, turnips and other vegetables. All of us kids had to help. We had a flock of chickens and a small herd of cows. We girls milked the cows. We had to get up very early to do the milking before we went to school.

When Mama accumulated a surplus of produce, one of my brothers would take off from school and drive Mama to the settlement where families lived who worked in the lumber mill. From the wagon she would peddle vegetables, butter, eggs and whatever else was in season. That's the way Mama helped Papa and they used the money as they saw fit. They didn't believe money should be left out for children to see. They didn't approve of that because it might encourage children to steal. It is good to trust a child but not put temptation in front of him. Papa kept the money in his pocketbook.

In the spring, Papa would ask Mama if she thought $150 would be enough money to borrow to get the crops started. They would decide how much they needed and the cows would be used for security on the loan. Papa would plant the main crop and then go back to his job with the lumber company. He was paid in scrip which he used at the company commissary.

Icy fondly described her first childhood home.

There was one big room about 14x16 that was used for cooking, eating, and sleeping. There was a fireplace in it and three beds, together with a long table and benches. There were no window panes. When you closed the slab windows,[1] it was dark inside. In this room, one bed was for my mother and father, and the other two for the smallest children. Two rooms like porches were on each side of the big room. One was a bedroom for the boys and the other for the girls. Each room had two beds. I slept three to a bed until I was grown and married.

---

[1] Slabs were sawed pieces of wood with bark on one side and smooth on the other. Years ago, particularly on log houses, they were cut to fit the windows as a type of shutter.

Papa built another home later when he was a "little better off." It had a bedroom for my parents, one for company and a separate room for cooking and eating. 'Course we would have to go through the cold wind to get to the kitchen because it was at the end of the porch. We used the porch for sitting and relaxing, 'specially when company came.

We children attended school only a mile or so from home. The seven grades were taught by young men and women who had acquired teaching certificates. Any person who could pass the test was given a permit to teach. My brother and I took the test but we didn't pass.

We walked to school but had to come home at noon to help Mama. We would finish cooking dinner, wash the dishes and go back to school. We all helped at noon and it didn't take us long to get the job done. Finally, we asked if we could take our dinner in a bucket. Papa said it was all right. So we would have biscuits and sometimes when we butchered, we'd have hogshead cheese. Everybody had syrup because we made syrup.

I remember one of our teachers was a married man with a family. He lived about twelve miles from school and he would walk home on Friday night and come back on Sunday night. During the week he stayed with the Banks family.

After I finished the seventh grade, I begged my father to let me go to the school in Cleveland, a town about ten miles away, to finish the eighth grade. So Papa sent me there for about two months. Then our little money gave out, and I had to come back home. My younger brother, Grady, wanted to go to school after the seventh grade, so bad. He was sent to school in Houston, where he finished high school and got a good job. Some of the younger children in the family finished the eighth grade and went on to high school, but I was needed at home to help Mama.

The fourteen children born between 1893 and 1917 to Effie and Barney Carnes were delivered by a midwife, Catherine Basoon, who was Barney's half-sister. Icy's tale about "where babies came from" was told with the candor and humor special to one who has lived more than eighty years.

When Catherine Basoon came it was a sure sign we children would be sent off to some of the neighbors and kinfolk to stay all night. We didn't know anything about what was happening.

We'd come home the next day or night and there would be a little baby.

Then when I was about fifteen, my sixth brother was born. Mrs. Basoon said, "Now Ila (she was my older sister) and Icy, you girls ain't gonna leave tonight. Your mother is gonna have that baby, and I'm gonna wait on her. I want you girls to stay here and I will tell you how they are born and everything."

She sat down and told us about it and we just didn't know what to think—but she thought it was time us girls were learning. We stayed that time when Mama had the baby. She didn't have a bit of trouble. It was just wonderful! From then on, must have been four or five more children born, we didn't have to leave home for the birthing.

It was easy to understand why young girls were so innocent when Icy told about what was customary when large families got together.

They would bring a bunch of children. We girls couldn't stay around when the mothers were talking. They would tell us, "You all go on to play." They would never talk in front of us and we weren't allowed to ask questions; so we went on to play. That's why we didn't know about many things until we were grown.

After I was older, I would go help at a neighbor's home when they had a baby. The first time I went to help a woman have her baby, it was my first cousins's wife. She had a doctor and I handed him the things he needed. I was never allowed to help the midwife when Mama's babies were born but, I could help the midwife or the doctor for other women.

The only time Icy spoke with a touch of irony in her voice was when she reviewed the tedious jobs that were necessary for their large family. Washing clothes was one of them. Thirteen of the fourteen children lived to adulthood. One little sister died at age four.

It seems like I was washing diapers most of my life. We also made soap which was used not only for laundry but everything else. All us girls used that soap when we washed our long hair. My sister and I have never cut our hair.

To make the soap we mixed lye, cracklings and water in a three-legged pot set out in the yard. A wood fire kept the mixture boiling. It was stirred until it started to thicken. Then we pulled the fire back and stirred some more until the soap was ready to pour in a pan and cover and then let it set overnight. The next morning it was cut into bars with a big butcher knife.

Washing clothes for fifteen people was often more than a day's job. Twice a week was more usual. The boys would fill four tubs with water. The wash pot was then filled and a fire built under it. The clothes were beat to get the dirt out by pounding on a wooden block using a wooden bat. Then we put the clothes in the pot to boil in the soap until they were clean. There were three tubs of rinse water.

At first we didn't have any clothesline. We just hung the clothes on the picket fence. Later years we had galvanized wire. If it was a bad day and the clothes didn't get dry we hung them around in the house on quilting frames. When it got cold, we'd build a fire in the fireplace and get up during the night and turn the clothes.

Mama and all us daughters spent hours cooking. Occasionally Papa would help. I started making biscuits when I was seven or eight. I'd stand on a stool to reach the table. I remember when Mama was in bed with a baby and before us girls got big enough, Papa would make the bread. We had a big old bread pan. I'll bet it held twenty-four biscuits. We would sift flour on a wooden tray and mix in our soda, salt, baking powder, milk and grease.

We would have biscuits for breakfast. Sometimes we would have bacon, and we'd have milk to drink--skim or buttermilk--'cause Mama used the cream to make butter. We would always say, "Thank you for the biscuit." If you took more than you ate at breakfast, you had to eat it at the next meal.

Icy laughed when she told me how she cheated when it was her turn to wash dishes.

When Ila and I were old enough, we'd take turns with the housework. One day I'd cook and wash dishes and Ila would make beds and sweep the floor. When I washed dishes, every pan that I possibly could, I'd soak. I'd put water in it and set it back. Then when it was my sister's turn to wash dishes, she

The Carnes Family.

would have to wash all the pans. Ila was so nice with everything—but just so I got by, that was all I was after.

Parching green coffee was another task that came my way.
You had to watch it every minute so it wouldn't burn. One time
when I wasn't watching it closely enough my father caught me.
"Dump (he used to call me Dump when I was little because I
was fat), if you let that coffee burn, I'll come and whip you." It
had to be parched just so. After it got cool you put it in the
coffee mill for grinding. Then you put it in the water in the
coffee pot and let it boil a little. My mother would always use
an egg shell to settle the grounds. People used to say, "Sister
Carnes, you make the best coffee!" We children didn't drink
coffee.

*Icy recalled how her mother spent some of her "peddling"
money on material and made all of the girl's dresses.*

My sister, Ila and I dressed alike. Mama had a sewing machine but no patterns. She would depend on pictures in a catalog. We girls would pick out the way we wanted our dresses made and Mama would cut a pattern. She made my brother's shirts and would often embroider on the sailor collar. Our family would dress up when we went to church or on some special occasion.

When we went to town to get our family picture taken we were really dressed up. There were eight children then. They were about a year apart. Mama and Papa sat in chairs in the front. Mama held one baby on her lap and Papa held the other one. We other children stood up. We had lots of fun when they took that picture. When we came back home Ila said to me, "You know, I don't think Mama is gonna have any more children, or they wouldn't have had that picture taken." But she was wrong. Mama had six more babies.

Many times Mama would be frustrated and she would fuss and get mad and say to Papa, "You oughtn't a-done that," and she would talk, talk, talk, but he would never cross her. I understood why Mama did that. She was ambitious. Never did I hear him cross her. He'd talk nice and kind and go on out to work. Mama would turn to us children and say, "If your papa would say just one word, I'd hush." But he never did quarrel with her.

Images of her mother are interwoven in Icy's stories of her youth.

Mama dipped snuff but Papa didn't smoke or chew or dip. A lot of men and women dipped snuff. Mama would buy snuff at the store with the groceries. She used the W. E. Garrett brand. Some people would dip snuff with a toothbrush. Some would go out in the woods and get a limb from a black gum bush, peel it, and chew it until it was soft. Then they'd use that to dip into the snuff box.

One time a cousin on my mother's side came over to visit and stole some snuff. Mama didn't scold the girl or accuse her but she didn't think it was right. She told the girl's mother and the girl's mother took care of the disciplining. She wouldn't steal her own mother's snuff but she did steal my mother's.

One time when I was in my teens, a man told my father, "Why don't you take those children to West Texas to pick cotton? You can make a livin' pickin' cotton." So we all went to Temple, Texas in a covered wagon. Mama had a very small baby. We carried our bedding and our stuff to cook with. We girls slept inside the wagon and the boys slept on a pallet outside. It was in the late summer. We all stayed well and had a good time.

We were paid about fifty cents a hundred. I was a poor hand to pick and one of my cousins said, "Put a lot of sand in your sack." I tried hard. I'd grab some sand and put it in my sack, but I never could bring my pounds up. Some could pick as much as three or four hundred pounds a day, but I never could do it. Papa would tell us to pick with the sun on our back, so it wouldn't be so hot. We picked cotton just that one season. The lumbering and saw mill life was more to my liking.

My father would cut logs and make the right-of-way for the dinkey.[2] He laid the track and everything. Six or seven men would lay the ties and the track for the log train to come through. Them days they used mules. They'd harness the mules to the flatbed hauling the lumber. We would go down and watch them but my father would never let us get too close because it was very dangerous--sometimes those heavy chains broke. They'd unload the logs in a pond and float them down to the mill.

When a family needed a fireplace built, all the neighbors would get together for a "chimney daubin'." The women would cook and the men would mix mud, moss, and water to make the chimney. The moss was put in to keep the mud from washing away. The fireplace would last for a long time. Sometimes they were used for cooking, but mostly for heat. We used pine cones to start the fires and bark to cook by.

My brothers would start the fireplace on cold mornings but we always had to help the boys in the field, so it evened out.

We were brought up to be Christians and we went to church whenever we could. When we went to church Mama and Papa sat in front on the wagon seat and we children sat in the back. When we got big enough, the older ones would walk 'cause we didn't live too far. We'd wear our best dresses.

Family, community, social, and religious activities were abundant.

---

[2] A small locomotive used to haul and shunt log cars.

We belonged to the Church of Christ. Once a year we had a protracted meeting [revival] and it would last a week. Everybody brought something for the preacher—two or three gallons of syrup, or lard, or bacon and whatever you had. That's the way we paid the preacher.

Later on, when we were better off, we'd have a little money to pay cash. The men would get together to see if they had enough. If one of the Brothers failed on his crop, and there wasn't enough money, we wouldn't have the meeting. Meetings would be on nights when the moon was full so people could see going home. We didn't have any lights on our wagons.

As Icy talked it was evident that social events where she could meet other young people were becoming more important to her.

We had fun at "candy breakin'" parties. We would put sticks of candy in a shoe box and open a little hole in the box. When you and your partner came along you drawed out two and if your sticks matched you could draw again until you made a misdraw. Then you would have to put your stick of candy back. You might end up with a stick and a half of candy.

We used to have cake walks too. We would pass a broom handle around in the yard among the party-goers. Someone would come out of the woods and shoot off a gun and if you had the broomstick in your hand when the gun went off, you would get the cake.

Parties and dances most often were held at neighborhood homes. I liked the dances best, though we girls couldn't go to dances alone. Mama would go with us. One of the boys would drive the wagon and Papa would stay home and keep the younguns. Not until we were about eighteen could we girls go alone. Then we'd get other young folks to go with us, but we had to be back at a certain time with the wagon. We would get a whippin' if we didn't come back when we were supposed to. We were not allowed to go out of the house during the dance.

We'd take all the beds down and take the furniture out and start dancing. The neighbor boys would play the fiddle and pick guitar and we'd have someone call the sets. We'd square dance and schottische and waltz and two-step. If we had a good caller and fiddler, I could dance all night long. My mother was a fine waltzer. I still think about those good days. We had the best time in the world!

Icy remembered a conversation with her mother that changed her life.

We were happy and we enjoyed being together. It just never dawned on me to marry until one day Mama and I were setting out rose bushes. Mama set her rose bushes out in the winter. She would put an iron rod in the ground, cut off a limb, put it in near the rod, and they would always grow. I wanted to put one here, and one over there, and Mama said, "Icy, you should fix you a bed—make your own bed of roses."

I thought that over and what Mama meant was I should be getting married. I was nineteen. I sat down and made my plans. I had boy friends and every one I had, I told him I was gonna marry him. And I didn't mean a word of it. I wrote letters to a semi-weekly farm newspaper. Young folks could write and get pen pals. I wrote and got several letters from boys and I'd answer. They wrote back asking if I wanted to get married and I'd say, "Oh yes, Oh yes! I had a lot of pictures from them. None had come to see me yet, but they wanted to.

Mama got into my letters one day and said, "Icy, let me tell you something. You're gonna have to quit this or else you're gonna be in trouble. Some of these boys might be expecting you mean what you say."

I got to thinking about it and concluded I should get married and have a home of my own. I could plant my flowers like I want. And that's what I done.

As she spoke Icy seemed to be enjoying again the excitement of courting when she was "nineteen, goin' on twenty." However, her father was still in control of her life. He determined who would come to see his daughter. This was apparent in Icy's recollections of Aaron Turner.

Aaron Turner wanted to make a date with me. The Turners lived on one side of the creek and we lived on the other. Papa didn't like this boy's daddy. He said Mr. Turner, who was a trustee at the Bear Creek school, was always meddling with our school.

Aaron told me he was gonna write me a letter and I knew that might cause a problem because the post office was in a separate room built onto our house. Papa was the postmaster.

The mail rider rode a horse ten miles to pick up the mail and take it to Cleveland. We had little boxes where we put the mail.

I watched when the mail came and when I got the letter from Aaron I saw Papa put the letter in his pocket. I said, "Papa, didn't I get a letter?" He said, "You get out of here or I'll give you a whipping." In another day or two, I asked again about the letter. Papa said, "Dump, I'm gonna give you this letter, but I don't want to ever hear of you answering it, or you'll get that whipping." I never answered it.

One night we were at church and Aaron Turner's daddy was preaching and Aaron was there too. We were all singing. I saw Papa peeking in the window. He wanted to see if I was with Aaron. But I wasn't. Papa had told me I couldn't go with him and I didn't give him no trouble. He didn't have to say anything else to me, but that sure broke up the courtship.

Then there was Willie Bradford. Willie lived at Splendore. He took me to church in a wagon he had borrowed. He was really in love with me! He wanted to get married but the First World War broke out and he had to go. He was sent to France and fought right on the firing line. A preacher's son from our town was with him at the front. He said Willie told the other boys there, "If I get killed, you tell my girl, Icy Carnes, about it. 'Cause I love her." Then the next shot he got killed. I'm glad he didn't know it, because by then I had already married Calvin.

When I was in the sixth grade at the Montag School, Calvin Banks started attending school there. They had always lived in the same area but the Banks children had gone to another school. Calvin's greatest trouble was he couldn't never remember where his lessons was at—that was his excuse! He would come ask me. We started writing little notes.

Our first date was a disappointment. Our church was having a meeting at the Montag School. Calvin's family belonged too. While we were having the meeting Calvin asked me if he could walk me home. I said he could.

My sister Ila (we called her Cricket), who was older than me, was there too. She was thinner than I was but we looked and dressed alike.

After the meeting, we were all standing out in front of the school. It was moonlight and we didn't have any gas light then. The folks were standing around and talking and when we all got ready to leave Calvin made a mistake and took my sister Ila by the arm and walked away. I walked home with my two other sisters. I said, "Let's go. He's taking Ila. I don't want a boy friend anyway."

Ila told me afterward, when they had walked on a little piece, Calvin said, "Oh, I made a mistake. I was going to walk with Icy! The next day at school he wrote me a little note saying he was sorry. We started going together off and on.

Calvin lived with his father and two sisters. His daddy told him he would pay his way to college, 'cause he wanted him to study and learn to make something out of himself. Mr. Banks had sent Calvin's two sisters to college and they were teachers. He said if Calvin wasn't going to study he couldn't just stay home. He had to go to work and earn his own bread. He preferred to go to work. He got a job working in a lumber mill making railroad ties.

I had other boy friends, but Calvin Banks always came back. He never gave up. We dated for two years. Then Calvin asked me to marry him and I said I would.

Icy conformed—did what was expected of her. She married the boy approved of by her family. She respected her father and made no attempt to change the plans he made for the newlyweds—even the decision about where they would spend their wedding night.

My folks liked Calvin. He was a good, home boy. He talked to Papa and told him, "Icy and me are thinking of getting married. I wondered what you have to say about it." Papa said, "Well it's a lifetime job."

Calvin picked the date. I remember how he put his finger on the 1917 calendar hanging on the wall and said we would be married on January 17, at 7:30 at night.

I recall the many gifts relatives, friends and neighbors gave us. The first was from the county judge. When Calvin rode to the county seat to get his marriage license, the judge who had known him for many years, said, "I'm not going to charge you for your license. I'm going to give it to you—it's a precious gift." It would have cost Calvin $1.50.

My mother made my wedding dress. It was light blue with a round collar and a gathered skirt. I wore high-topped button shoes. Didn't have a hat, veil or gloves. The preacher married us by lamplight on the porch of our home. After the ceremony everyone crowded into the kitchen-dining room and ate the supper Mama had prepared. The wedding was just like my sister Ila's, who was married about six months earlier.

In those days neighbors and friends, as well as relatives, would shivaree the bride and groom on their wedding night. They would ring bells, pound on tubs, rattle tin cans, shoot guns and make lots of noise around where the newlyweds were until the groom came outside. Then they would take him off and keep him 'til nearly daybreak.

After our marriage when the folks started leaving for their homes, Papa said, "Now they're plannin' big on shivareeing you and Calvin. You stay here tonight and there won't be any shivaree. So we stayed at my home that night. The next morning one of my brothers hitched up the mules to the wagon and drove us to Cleveland where we spent two nights and days with Ila. Then we went back to my parents' home, gathered together the things that had been given to us to start housekeeping. I didn't have a "hope chest." Mother gave us a mattress, dishes, sheets, pillows and two quilts. Calvin's father gave us a bedstead, and his sister contributed a little wood stove and an iron kettle. Someone else gave us several chairs and an old table.

My brothers moved us three miles back in the woods to the two-room house Calvin had built. It was near the saw mill where Calvin worked for $1.50 a day. He had saved $60 but had to use very little of it to begin our married life. Our needs were simple. We bought a big sack of bolted cornmeal for fifty cents It lasted a month. Neither one of us drank coffee and we didn't know about tea then. My mother provided us with milk and vegetables. My folks shared their harvest of sweet potatoes and black-eyed peas.

Meat was plentiful. Calvin was an expert when it came to butchering. Hogs ran wild in the forest, feeding on acorns that fell from the trees. When we needed pork, the men would get their guns and go out hunting pigs. They took along a horn which they'd blow when they had shot a hog. When we women heard the bellow from the horn, we would get the water hot so when the men came with the hog, they could throw it into the boiling water. Then Calvin would take over. After the hog was skinned and the leaf fat peeled off, the hog would be cleaned with cold salt water.

We used every bit of the meat except the ear drum. It was said that if you ate the ear drum, it would kill you. We made sausage. The meat was smoked slowly for nine days. We used green hickory wood for the smoking. We had hams and bacon. One of our favorite meals was biscuits, syrup, bacon with gravy and onions. We really ate good.

Calvin's daddy had cows and we killed a beef about six times a year. We'd smoke that also. We divided with the neighbors.

We had peach and pear trees too but we had to dry the fruit in the sun to keep it for winter. In later years when we had jars, we would can the fruit.

Family dependency, for companionship as well as material things, continued through the early years of the young couple's married life. With the Carnes and Banks relatives nearby, breaking family ties was difficult. Icy emphasized this as she continued.

Almost every weekend we would walk over to see my parents or we would visit with Calvin's father and sisters. Calvin's mother died when he was a child.

When the mill ran out of timber and the lumber operation moved about twenty miles from Cleveland, Calvin and I decided to go back to my father's farm. My father had a place and he wanted us to move into that and help him, and we all farmed together. We did mighty good. Calvin's father was gettin' old. He had a nice herd of cows and he needed Calvin to help him. The cows would just run in the woods on land that belonged to the Foster Lumber Company. They didn't charge anything. Calvin's folks had 265 acres and he would divide that among his four children.

Later on we built a house of our own on the Banks' farm. It was built with one by twelve foot planks that were planed slick. It was our first home that wasn't made of logs. We had a mud chimney, and a porch and a kitchen. We thought it was really nice. We kept our food in a "safe." It was like a screened cupboard. The back was solid. For a long time we didn't have screen doors, just wooden doors. We needed the safe to keep the flies from our food. We lived in that house for eleven years.

It was December 1925 when we bought our first car. We borrowed $495 from Calvin's father to pay for it and we both worked and paid back every penny. At night we would light our lantern and go out and look at the car.

We were married ten years before our first child was born. We called him Loy Cullen. Six years later a second son, Joe, was born, followed in fifteen months by son Doyle.

Banks

This was the beginning of an era in Icy Bank's life when she had to be aggressive and persistent with other people. It seemed totally out of character in one way, but totally logical in another. Someone she loved needed help—Doyle.

Doyle was born at home, just after midnight. Shortly after the doctor left, he started crying. He cried all night long. The next morning Calvin and my sister took the baby to Fostoria. We knew it wasn't right for a baby to cry so hard for so long. When they got to the doctor's office he stopped crying. The doctor examined him and thought he would be all right. But he wasn't. He had a paralyzed right arm, and his legs were deformed and almost lifeless.

The intensity and tone of Icy's voice as she described her son's condition and her first attempts to make him well were indications of what later became her obsession. There were hundreds of visits to doctors to find out what could be done to help Doyle. Icy continued working alongside her husband and did not neglect her other children.

Mama thought there was something wrong when the baby couldn't reach for the rattle we got him. He would topple over when we propped him up on pillows. That's when we started taking him to doctors. The baby specialist in Houston told us about having polio the very night he was born. He gave us medicine to give Doyle and said to keep him out in the sunshine as much as we could. I put a pallet out in the sun. I did everything they told me to and he didn't seem to get much better.

Some other doctors examined him one day and he had a fever. They put him on a blanket and tried to make him crawl. He had learned to crawl, but they worked with him so long he was all tired out. I said to them, "Do you know, or can you tell me what to do for my baby?" They said, "We don't know. You take him home and do what your family doctor tells you to do." And that's what I done.

Every night I would rub his legs good and his back and arms. I built him a little pen. I went out in the woods and got a pole and peeled it and I'd put that in the pen so he could stand near it.

My neighbors would come, first one and then another, and tell me what to do. One neighbor said to wash the baby in dishwater. I done everything they told me. By then, he could walk a little if I held him.

I built him a high chair. I got pieces of plank and fixed it so he would be right up even with the table when he ate. He learned to feed himself with his little hands. Course I had to keep that chair scrubbed.

Finally we ordered him a walker with four wheels. He began to walk in that. When he got so he could sit alone pretty good, I built him a little low chair and I would set him in that and carry him around where I was working.

One fall, Calvin and I and the three boys were out in the woods cutting our firewood; Doyle was sitting in his little chair. All of a sudden he got up out of his chair and walked around it. Oh, I was tickled to death! I called his daddy to come and see. And do you know, Doyle got up and walked around that chair again. And that's the way it came about. He was almost three years old.

After her son learned to walk, Icy continued her daily care and support. When Doyle was ready for first grade she related how the principal of the school reacted.

"I don't believe we can take him in school here," he said.

"I'll tell you one thing," I replied, "Doyle is going to school somewhere. If he can't go to school here, I'll take him to Cold Springs. We'll move up there where we can send him to school."

After a while the principal relented and told us we could bring him to school and they would try. So Doyle started in school there. He made straight A report cards all the way through!

When Doyle finished high school, his counselors suggested he work in an upholstery or tire shop. They kept suggesting some kind of trade. I said, "You want him to do that kind of work? He can't use his hands that well. With his grades he should go to college."

The college at Huntsville, Texas required extensive entrance exams. Doyle passed them, and I found him a place to live. I brought him home weekends, cleaned his clothes, and took him back on Sunday evening with enough food to last the week.

My next challenge came when Doyle wanted to transfer to Texas A&M. Unfortunately, one dean of admissions was tactless and blunt when Doyle said he wanted to be a petroleum engineer. He said, "You can't pass the tests you will need to enter this college." I thanked the dean and left. My oldest son Loy was with Doyle and me. He said, "Mother, what are we going to do?" I said, "We're going to take Doyle over to another dean and he's going to help us." Loy said, "Doyle, are you worried?" Doyle said, "No, I'm not." I said, "And I'm not either."

So we talked to another dean and he was very helpful. He suggested that Doyle study electrical engineering because there wasn't so much walking required. Doyle thought that was a good idea so he took some entrance exams and passed them and started school there.

Doyle received his bachelor of science degree in electrical engineering and went on to get his master's degree. He got a good job as an engineer, got married and became a father. He has a lovely home and family and proved to everybody that he could make it despite his handicap.

Icy had won, and survived, her toughest battle.

~~~~~~

As a child and as a woman, Icy Carnes Banks played many roles. No one could have carried them off with more determination, grace and good humor. Calvin Banks died February 8, 1980, after seven years of illness. During that time Icy was always near, making the most of their days together. She believed in what her father had said to Calvin so many years ago, "It's a lifetime job."

~~~~~

Icy Carnes Banks was ninety when she died in August, 1986, at her son's home in Wyoming. She was buried in Cleveland, Texas, where she had spent most of her life. Her three sons, Loy, Joe and Doyle survive her.

Lois Gray Barton

ROOSTER AND CAKE

Lois Gray Barton

In the summer of 1980, Lois Gray Barton lived in the University Terrace Good Samaritan Retirement Village in Las Cruces, New Mexico where I interviewed her. When I entered the living room of her small apartment, I felt I was stepping back in time to the late nineteenth century. The cherry wood Duncan Phyfe table, the Queen Anne chairs and a china cupboard, among other pieces of period furniture, provided an appropriate setting for conversation with this charming, dignified woman born in 1886.

Mrs. Barton insisted her life had been uneventful and there really wasn't much to talk about. As she began to reminisce it was apparent her life story would be interesting. Her background and lifestyle were quite different from many of the other women interviewed, so the comparison provides a broader historical picture of women born in the late 1880s. Here is her story:

I was born ninety-four years ago in a little town in Texas called Overton, about thirty miles east of Dallas. My father died when I was about five years old. I vaguely remember him. My mother was only 32. I remember my wonderful mother very clearly.

I was the second oldest of the four surviving children. Two children died so there were eight years between my older sister and me. My brother, the youngest, was a baby when our father died. Mother reared us herself. She was a very retiring woman and never remarried. We owned our home and it had a very large yard. Mother encouraged the children in the neighborhood to come to our place to play instead of letting us go away. If it was like it is now, I know my mother would have made money doing what she did. Perhaps she felt inadequate, young

"

as she was with four children to raise. It seems to me now that she didn't want us to get out of her sight.

I had a very happy childhood, even though I didn't have a father. We didn't have a swimming pool so my mother would take us walking in the woods. We had springs and streams all around our house. We would go [to the stream] and take old dresses. I won't say we went swimming 'cause none of us could swim then but we went in the water and had fun splashing around.

I remember a perfectly darling birthday party when I got a tea set to play with. It was the largest tea set I ever saw. That evening we went to the Overton's house. They were very prominent—the town was named after them. Some very dear friends of my mother were there, women her age. A lady asked me what I had for dinner and I said "rooster and cake." They all laughed. I embarrassed mother when I blurted that out. Mother raised chickens and said she wanted to eat that rooster because he was so big, so she baked it for my birthday dinner.

Mrs. Barton talked about family relationships in her youth and how her mother guided and controlled their lives.

We were a very closely knit family. My mother wanted us home. We were happy but it seemed there was never anything very humorous or eventful happening. Mother didn't allow me to go out with boys until I was sixteen and went away to school. She just didn't like for me to. I had friends—worlds of friends. We had parties in the evening and played out in the yard.

She talked briefly, and with some emotion, about her younger brother and how his life was so different from her sisters'.

Now, when I think about it, I believe it made a difference in his life because he was the only son and didn't have a father. I thought nothing about it at the time. He didn't go out and work when he was young to help my mother financially. He attended a business college in Dallas. He died in his early fifties.

After graduating from high school Lois Gray went to North Texas State University in Denton. She described her college days humbly and continued on about careers for women, women working outside the home, and their place in society.

They didn't have dormitories at college. We lived in a private home. I was with another girl from my home town. I'm not quite sure what classes I took. I know I wanted to go to the Baylor School for Girls and I have always regretted that I didn't get to go there. It wasn't the big Baylor University. I'm not sure that it is still going.

I hadn't even thought about getting a job while I was in college. I think that's the way everybody felt. Women didn't work. I'm past ninety. That's the way it was. My sister graduated from a music conservatory and taught music. My other sister married when she was about 20. I was ten or eleven then. She lived in Oklahoma Territory. That's what they called Oklahoma then. She died there about ten years ago.

There was no enthusiasm in her voice when she discussed Women's Suffrage.

About 1916 and '17, somewhere along in there, some were talking about women voting. My sister and I were not interested. Living in a small town, we didn't hear much about Woman Suffrage. We read a lot. My mother read and my family loved to read—my brother too. I was familiar with some of the articles through reading about getting the vote for women. Neither of my sisters was interested in the movement. We were interested only in public affairs and politics in our town.

I do remember when the law was passed giving women the vote in 1920. I was married then and my husband wanted me to vote. I was real sick so someone had to come from another town. I think it was Henderson, Texas. This official brought me papers to sign. I guess it was to register for voting. I remember sitting up in bed and I really didn't know about what I did. But it happened and I voted.

I taught school in a little country town in Texas for a year or so. I don't remember needing any certification to teach. I just went and taught. The school was a little old wooden building. There were desks and everybody came to school. Eight grades and I taught everything. Must have been at least twenty of all ages. I remember one great big tall fellow. I didn't have to take care of the stoves or do the janitor work like some of the other teachers. The son of one of the trustees did that. I didn't do a thing but teach.

*The Gray home in Overton, Texas where Lois Barton
spent her childhood.*

*Mrs. Barton spoke matter-of-factly about her courtship and
wedding and the early years of her marriage.*

The boy from Overton that I was going with, Virgil Barton,
was in school in Georgetown, Texas when I was in Denton. I
went with several boys. Virgil was two or three years older than
I was but we had been in the same high school. We wrote to
each other when we were in college and sometimes he would
come to Denton to see me. He was a member of the Kappa
Sigma Fraternity.

Virgil and I went together for a long time. I never gave
anyone else much thought. He traveled by horse and buggy to
see me. It must have been fifty or sixty miles. He would spend

Sunday with me. We became engaged in early spring and married in December. We were married fifty-five years.

I was married at home. My mother wanted it that way. Some of my friends were so disappointed I didn't have a church wedding, but my mother said, "No." We had quite a number of guests. Our living room was large and it was practically filled. I wore a long white silk dress my mother made. It had smocking, a high neck and long sleeves. It was perfectly beautiful! My mother made a good many of my dresses.

We lived with my husband's parents in Texas for about fifteen months after we were married. They had a very large twelve or fourteen room two-story home. They were so nice. Mrs. Barton and I became good friends, and always were.

I wanted a home of my own so we rented a house and later we bought our own place. My mother had owned her home and every one in our family eventually owned their home. It was instilled in us to own your home. I don't know why. Some business friend of my husband once said, "Don't buy a home. I advise you to rent." But my husband and I didn't feel that way.

It was apparent that women were not involved in actual financial transactions and other family business, but their opinions and reactions played an important part in setting family goals.

My husband's family owned a general mercantile store. Virgil was in business with his father for a while. He also worked in Tyler at a wholesale place, but his father wanted him back so he went back several times and worked for him.

Tyler was a little town like Overton. But Tyler has grown. We came to Las Cruces, New Mexico in 1929. Tyler was a lovely little town and it became a city when they discovered oil. Oil came down there in 1930. We didn't own any land there. Had we been living there my husband would have bought property because he was that kind of man. But we didn't and I have always been a little disappointed. Some of my friends there are worth worlds of money today!

One time when I was complaining, my oldest son said to me, "But mother, there are a lot of broken homes back there. You don't know what might have happened. Daddy might have fallen in love with somebody else. Maybe, we better be glad that we were out here." That was the way some things happened back there. But I was a little disappointed. I still am.

Barton

The nostalgia was sad to observe when Mrs. Barton talked about her life in Texas and their moving to New Mexico.

My husband's brother lived in Portland, Oregon. When he found out we were leaving Texas, he wanted us to move to Portland. My husband didn't find anything he liked there. When he heard of this opening in Las Cruces, he decided to move here.

Mr. Barton worked for Anderson-Clayton, the Houston cotton people. He was manager of their business here. Our little town in Texas.... Well, people had moved away. That was before the oil came. My husband could have continued in the mercantile business but he sold out and Anderson-Clayton offered him this position. We sold our home in Texas. I had such a lovely home. My mother left the home place to me and we had a home built on it. I always grieved about leaving it.

The majority of the homes were one story. Some were two story but they were large homes, maybe three or four bedrooms. Most were built of lumber, not many brick homes. Mine was three bedrooms but we never did get the bathroom all fixed. We didn't have indoor plumbing.

We lived in two different homes in Las Cruces. The house on Reymond was build by a Mr. Maese. He sold it to Mr. Hoagland and Hoaglands sold it to us. We moved into that house on June 10, 1930. Realtors sold the place in 1979. They came to me on June 10, of that year and I signed the deeds away. It was quite a coincidence. I have grieved terribly. I am still heartsick about it.

We came to New Mexico by automobile. I remember we bought our first car in 1916. It was a Dodge. I don't know how many Dodge cars we bought until one time I was going to drive to Tennessee to visit and was taking my daughter and youngest son with me. The Dodge broke down and it was a new car. We'd only had it a year. The mechanics found a piece that caused the problem and gave it to my husband. It was rusty. I don't know what part it was. I didn't know about that. We were told the Dodge people would make it good and they didn't. We never bought another Dodge. They gave us something, I'm sure, but not what my husband thought they should.

Her voice reflected pride when she spoke of her children and deep sadness when she recalled her daughter's death.

Barton

We had a daughter and three sons. All four were born in Texas. We didn't have a hospital in those days but I always had a doctor and a nurse come to our home when the children were born. The nurse stayed with me. They kept me in bed more than ten days. I remember they wouldn't even let me get my arms out. I think it is very sensible the way they do now. Some mothers leave the hospital in a day or so. My first child was a son who was born the last of September. My daughter was born second when my son was six years old. She was a darling, darling little girl all her life; such a lovely person. She is dead now.

It was very apparent, as Mrs. Barton talked about the past, that her family and home were most important to her at every passage within her life. Before I left she wanted me to see the bed her mother had brought with her from the South when she moved to Texas over a hundred years ago. The bed was the focal point of her delightful bedroom. The large "four-poster" with a wide, curved headboard stood majestically on one side of the room. Pictures stood on the top of the matching chest of drawers. Other framed photographs and snapshots of Gray and Barton family ancestors, as well as other relatives and friends, covered the walls.

She pointed proudly to a framed certificate on the wall in her hallway. It proclaimed Lois Gray Barton as a Daughter of the American Revolution and a descendent of Josiah LeGrande, a soldier who fought in the American Revolution. Mrs. Barton was quick to explain that a cousin had searched the Congressional Archives and discovered that the certificate should have read "Captain Josiah LeGrande."

"I live with memories and my pictures," she said.

Upon leaving, I felt I should courtesy and say to this dignified woman, "Thank you, Lady Barton, for sharing your memories."

~~~~~~

Lois Gray Barton died October 22, 1982, and is buried in the Masonic Cemetery, Las Cruces, New Mexico beside her husband of fifty-five years. Her son, J.R. Barton is retired and lives in Santa Fe. Her other son, W. H. Barton, is also retired and lives in Uvalde, Texas.

~~~~~~

Elsie Chavez Chilton

$\mathcal{A}$S IT WAS IN CHIVA TOWN

Elsie Chavez Chilton

When I interviewed Elsie Chavez Chilton in 1983, she was active in community affairs and cared for her ninety-nine year old mother. Although a victim of muscular dystrophy, she had a positive outlook on life. She enjoyed recalling how it was in the sleepy little town of Las Cruces, New Mexico before the turn of the century.

When I was a girl there were no dams in Las Cruces. Whenever there was a flash flood up on the mountains, we would have a tremendous amount of water running down this way. Of course, there were natural arroyos that ran. It was very exciting for us and quite scary. Sometimes some of the homes were swept away.

The house where I was born on Tornillo is still standing. I do remember the house where we were raised, which is on the corner of Court and Mesquite. In later years there was a psychologist's office there. We had a big house. At that time, since the town was so sparsely populated, they built a house on each corner of the block so each block had only two houses. There was a vastness of brush, mesquite bushes, lizards and what have you. So we weren't crowded or close.

There were four houses in our area. Juan Apodoca, retired Las Cruces fire chief, is still living in the house on Las Cruces Avenue.[1]

---

[1] Mr. Apodaca reported the actual age of the house is unknown, but it is constructed of 'long adobe' bricks (8"x16"), which makes it a very old building. Because of extensive remodeling throughout the years, the home is not eligible for the National Register of Historic Places.

During World War II one of the houses was known to be a house of ill repute.[2] It is on East Court. When we were children we used to hear tell about it. Beyond our street was the city dump where people would go rabbit hunting.

We used to have a big dormitory room in our house for the five boys in our family. There were two of us girls. The boys would go out, I guess you would call it grubbing, for something to burn in the stove they had in their big room. They would get those mesquite roots, or tires or whatever else they could find and burn it in the big stove. We would have a roaring fire for a while and we were too hot. Then when the fire went out we would be cold again. Sometimes we would bundle up and go outside and play to keep warm. Mother would get up real early and go down to the leniero [man who sold wood] for wood for the stove in the kitchen. For a quarter she would get a tub full of wood and then she would have a nice warm fire going by the time we got up to dress. When we got out of school the sun would be shining and it wouldn't be so cold.

Food, so readily accessible today, was not so simply acquired before the days of pasteurization, refrigeration, frozen foods and chemicals for preservation. Mrs. Chilton told about what they did in the Southwest in the late Twenties and early Thirties to feed their families.

In the winter they used to come down from Chiva Town with goats they would butcher. Hogs too would be butchered. They would share. There was some refrigeration then but most people on the east side didn't have it. You could smell the raw meat from blocks away and everybody would gravitate to where the matanza [slaughtering] was. People would buy or give. It was a sort of give and take. When we butchered we would give to the neighbors and when they butchered they would share with us – chicharrones [fried pork skins], and carne adovada [pork meat], and whatever else there was.

---

[2] Carlos Sanchez, the current owner provided this information. "It has been remodeled. The house had lots of bedrooms and many doors on the back, opening to the outside. There was a bar in one of the large rooms and a big diningroom where they served meals for those who stayed overnight. Cowboys from the ranches went there when they came to town. There was a place in the back for their horses."

Chiva Town was several acres located up on the high place that is now Solano—all that area. The goats and the herders lived there in very, very small huts—makeshift places. They would milk the goats, sell the milk and the cheese and butcher some of the goats. They would come down to the lower part of town to sell it. We also had vegetable venders coming from Old Mesilla. They would have whatever was in season—corn, squash, tomatoes, beans or peas. They had the packing sheds over here by the depot where they would ship cantaloupes, cabbage, lettuce and onions. We always had lots of whatever was in season. We would dry chile, squash, and apples. Everything was dried instead of frozen.

Chiva Town still existed in the early Thirties. There were dairies by then. We never did drink the goat milk. We were just too squeamish. We had milk delivered or used canned milk. As we got into the Thirties we had more Anglo people here and we moved ahead.

Mrs. Chilton was most knowledgeable when she reviewed how the Depression in 1929 and the early 1930s affected the people in the Southwest.

In some ways the depression was sort of a good thing. There was aid or assistance for some people who had never had any kind of help before. Also, it was kind of gradual. My father was not always employed. He did masonry work, plastering, home building and everything like that. Las Cruces was never a booming town. People would buy a house and just remodel it themselves. Those who used to have money and those who never had it, were all in the same boat. A lot of the children who lived out in the country would ride horses to school and bring their butter or eggs and try to sell them to the teachers or whoever would buy them. They were trying to help out their families. Everybody wore hand-me-downs or just wore their clothes until there was no more wear in them. I wouldn't say that it hurt too much because none of us had very much anyhow.

Elsie Chilton explained that her point of view of this time period was that of a native. Her memories were of a time before newcomers moved into the Mesilla Valley.

I do know that those who did have money in the banks lost it all. The people who were born and raised here owned all the land. My father, Epefaniro Chavez, used to own a farm. If you go to an old map of Picacho you will see that the Chavez's owned all of Picacho. It was settled by the Chavez family. We didn't have much irrigation. The people who came in had money. They bought the land very cheaply. My father had acres and acres. I think Mr. Newberry wound up with his farm. They got all the peach trees my father had planted. After that my father got out of farming.

My mother Guadalupe Triviz, was born in the village of Doña Ana on December 12, 1883. She was baptized Guadalupe because December 12 is the feast day of Our Lady of Guadalupe. She and my father lived in Picacho when they were first married and that's where the older children were born. I've heard tell about how my mother used to have to cross the river. She still shudders with fear when she thinks of it. When the river was too high and swift, my father would put her, the children and all mother's satchels on horses. One time mother was having a baby and they sent word for my father to come but there was no way for him to get across. There were no bridges. He had to go a long way down the valley. By the time he got there, a day or two later, mama already had the baby.

At that time there was a lot of bartering. That was pre-depression and I was such a small child I don't remember too much about it, but I know they got along just fine. When the depression hit we were already living in town. We had no money to lose because we had no money in the bank. We did have hard times—especially the families whose fathers didn't have a steady income. I had uncles who had steady incomes. They were ditch riders. One was at Leasburg Dam and one at Mesilla Dam. Other uncles were army veterans and they had steady jobs at Fort Bayard. No matter how small it was, if it was a steady income it meant a lot. Since my father was self-employed that was worse. We managed somehow. Also there was the NYA [National Youth Administration] and the WPA [Works Progress Administration]. But my father didn't work for the WPA.

My father was a dreamer. He was always treasure hunting. He resorted to placer mining in Orogrande during the depression. He had some claims over in Orogrande that were taken away during the war. He had a little lake and he put together a small conveyor and every once in a while they would hit a vein. I remember seeing really beautiful nuggets. He used to make tie pins. My daughter still has one of them. He would put little tiny bits of gold in some of the lockets. It was all very fascinating. He brought home a lot of turquoise. All our doors had doorstops of big old rocks of turquoise. At that time Indian jewelry and turquoise were not popular here. Nor were cowboys. The Indians from Gallup used to come and peddle for rummage. I would keep little children's rings and bracelets to give at birthday parties. If a boy gave a girl a turquoise bracelet that was yuk, not good at all. We got by some of the bad years with my father doing the mining and jewelry making. One time he went to La Luz and worked for a man who had a mine.

Those were the "The Grapes of Wrath" years. Incidentally, Mesquite Street was a highway then and people traveling West from Oklahoma and other states would camp there when their vehicles broke down. Sometimes they camped there for weeks. They would litter and go from house to house on the street always borrowing things which we knew they couldn't pay back. We would wind up helping them. They didn't have money to fix their cars. Somehow they would get help and eventually leave Las Cruces.

They had the same problem in Orogrande. My father was so generous he would help them out with gasoline, groceries, or whatever they needed and charge it to his account at the store. The lady at the post office and grocery store at Orogrande saw everything. She would say, "Mr. Chavez, I'm going to keep that money and send it to your family. Don't be sending any more people over here to get gasoline or groceries on your account. The money you get from the gold that you mine doesn't go that far." That was a big help for our family when she took to handling my father's account.

My mother always used to say, "Casa de herrero azadon de palo," which means, "In the home of the blacksmith, wooden spoons." A long time ago, my mother's father was a blacksmith. They used to fashion the silverware also.

To get to Orogrande, my father used to take a shortcut through the mountains in his little fliver. I suppose that is almost the way they go across now. Sometimes he would have to go by way of El Paso. His mine was somewhere between El Paso and Alamogordo. Where his mine was has been closed for a long time. I don't think they allow anybody in there now.

We had a lot of boys from the East and everywhere working in the CCC camps around here. Where there are young boys and young girls they are going to meet. Some of those young men married our local girls—and some that didn't, but should have. We had a lot of work done by the CCC camp boys—Jornada Range was one area. I used to go with the one of the big shots with the camp. I would go over there and have dinner where the officials had dinner. My friend showed me all the fence that they had built. I don't know what they were fencing in but they built miles and miles of fence. I remember my brother went to Vista Viento in California. He got himself into a CCC camp and we were delighted. My folks got $25 a month that summer as a result of his working in the camp. Then for a short time, my father worked as a "pusher" at a camp in Radium Springs. Can you imagine that! That's what the boys used to call him. In the camps they called the supervisors that because they used to push the boys to do the work. That was soon over and he had to resort to his other jobs.

The conversation turned to education, segregation and how and what they were taught in the public schools in the early 1920's. Elsie Chavez Chilton's words were revealing, and tinged with a touch of regret, when she talked about the transition from her Spanish customs and way of speaking to what was expected of children when they started school.

There was segregation, but not only because the Spanish-speaking population was on the east side and the English-speaking population was on the west side. It was not as we know the west side now. Then the dividing line was on Alameda and Reymond Streets. There were not so many schools. Naturally, all the Spanish-speaking children would go to the school in their area—which was the Lucero School. We didn't have any kindergarten. People spoke Spanish at home so, when it was time to go to school, the children had to go into what they called a primer first grade and then they went into [the regular] first grade. At that time the teachers were so intent on teaching them to speak English that they forbade them to speak Spanish. The children would be out on the school yard and the minute the teacher would approach, why everybody would hush because they were speaking the only way they could—in Spanish.

Also, the teachers had the boys in one area and the girls in another.

We had some Black people, just a very, very few. I had already learned English from neighbors when we were in California so I was something of a novelty. The teachers used to keep me in at recess to sort of pump me. I guess they just wanted to hear a child speak English. They were tired of all the Spanish-speaking kids. Anyway, they would name us in English. They took away our Spanish names. My name, Elisa, became Elsie, my brother, Edwardo, became Edward or Eddie and Samuel became Sammy and so on down. To this day we have our English names but my mother still calls us by our Spanish names.

What the father, the undisputed head of the family, said was to be strictly obeyed. Elsie Chilton's honesty in recalling her mother's way of dealing with this, as well as justifying what the cotton-picking children did, is pleasantly refreshing.

My father would never take us out of school to work. He always said the best inheritance he could leave us was an education. We were not allowed to leave school and pick cotton. But, my father was not always in town. My mother would give in to us. Some of our cousins used to go pick cotton during Thanksgiving and holidays when school was let out. On occasions the students were dismissed or allowed—not counted absent—if they had to go pick cotton. We were some of the very few who stayed in school. Many students were out having fun. Whether they were truly picking cotton or not, they still stayed out of school. We would pick cotton on weekends and holidays and be real tickled to be earning some money. During holidays four of us children would come home with maybe $2.50 or three dollars. We could buy flannel for fifteen cents a yard. My mother would make flannel shirts and different pieces of clothing for us. We were proud that we had earned money.

Elsie Chilton's comments about disease, doctors, childbearing and health problems in the Spanish-speaking community were revealing. She described her important role as liaison with humility and wit.

Guadalupe Triviz Chavez and her children.

On the eastside there resided a Dr. Johnson. He was a Godsend because he was not so intent on getting rich, which he knew he couldn't do there. He was hard of hearing and had a hearing instrument but he was a real good doctor. I don't know how he did it but I think everybody who ever went to him got the same kind of pink pills. But they worked. I used to be a sort of spokesperson for the neighborhood because I guess my talent was talking. If anyone wanted a paper filled out, I would be the one who did it. Or, if going to the doctor, I would go with them. I remember coming home from the doctor one time and everybody surrounding me. It was very odd because the doctor had sent me home to keep on doctoring this child. I had to syringe the ear where he had an infection. You know the stuff was kind of gruesome but I was proud to be able to do it. He was that sort of a doctor. Instead of having them come and go, he would instruct somebody in the family on what to do. Of course, that came in handy the next time.

The other doctors were, Dr. Allison, Dr. Sexton, Dr. McBride, and Dr. Lane. They all came [to Las Cruces] because of health problems. Dr. McBride's wife and Dr. Lane had tuberculosis.

Most of the native women had midwives when they had babies. In fact, all of the children in our family were delivered by a midwife. Even my first child was born at home because they didn't have a hospital yet. They were putting together the old McBride Hospital but somebody had told me it wasn't so good. Plans had been made for me to stay home so I did. My other children were delivered at the McBride Hospital and the other hospital when it was built.

The time her family went to California was still vivid in Elsie Chilton's memory. That trip away from New Mexico made a lasting impression.

I remember when we went to California my mother had five or six children. We stayed in California one year. We lived in Santa Barbara which was a millionaire's haven. We belonged to the parish that had a Catholic school and everybody just showered attention and everything on us. They couldn't do enough for us. They had our tonsils yanked out whether we needed them out or not. They sent us to camp and they just did everything for us. In one year's time we learned English. We just loved being in Santa Barbara. But, my mother was pregnant and wanted to come back to New Mexico to have her baby so here we came. Living in California was quite an experience. My father had gone over there to work. I don't know why he decided to go to California in the first place, there were so many of us.

At an early age, Elsie Chilton assumed family responsibilities that she handled with grace and strength. Being a bilingual person at the intersection of two cultures was not an easy task for a young woman.

After we got back from California my sister died. I always say I was taking care of my parents and my family after her death. My sister, who was twelve years old when she died, was a very intelligent child. When we were in Santa Barbara she was the one who enrolled us in school. She took us on the street car and did things for the Sisters and ran errands. My mother used to rely on her tremendously so when she was gone I remember mother used to say she had lost her right arm. I took it literally and wondered how come my mother is telling this when she knows, it is very obvious, she still has her right arm. After that I sort of took over running errands and speaking for the family. I would take them to the doctor, enroll them in school, do the shopping and different things that parents usually do.

Mrs. Chilton laughed when she told about her experience with delousing.

The year we came back from California, I was in the first grade. I was a very friendly person. I used to love to put my arms around everybody and my brothers would be so mad at me. They knew there were a lot of cooties or lice all over the school because the teachers used to periodically pump some kind of a disinfectant on us. With all my hugging, I did get some lice and I had to be deloused. In those days parents didn't object to anything the school did to the children. Goodness, if anybody was to do that nowadays, parents would just raise the roof. 'Course, it was more or less a necessity, and people accepted it. It was a lot better than picking out the lice, I suppose. It just makes me sick to think about it. My mother was horrified when she heard about it, but nevertheless, I did pick up some lice and she was glad the school was doing the delousing. My brothers used to get real irritated because they were afraid I would bring them home.

The words just seem to flow when Elsie Chilton reminisced about recreation and what the young people did for entertainment in the mid-Twenties.

There were a lot of family things, baptisms, confirmations. weddings and anniversaries. There were very few public places and in those days my mother didn't like for me to go to public places. I used to sneak out once in a while, but with five brothers in town I couldn't get away with too much. We used to collect a quarter or fifty cents and rent a hall—like the KC Hall which is where the electric company is now. We would have a small band with a piano player, no orchestra or big deal. Maybe, a nickelodeon. And we would have a dance.

There used to be public places to go. They called one "El Indio." An Indian man owned a great big hall and he would have dances there. I would have liked to go to dances forever! But, my mother didn't like that at all, so I would sneak over there for an hour or two whenever I could.

When the National Guard boys went to Las Vegas [New Mexico] every summer, occasionally they would have street dances. At the Armory, where the politicians would give speeches, you would sleep through the speeches and then go to the dance afterward.

Later on in the Thirties, when I was older, there would be a lot of school activities and we would have more to do. At the Rio Grande Theater home talent would perform and at the Loretto Academy they had Comedias [Comedies].

Mrs. Chilton had many pictures in her mind of the buildings in Las Cruces as she remembered them.

The buildings were all old in the late Thirties and early Forties. They started remodeling them to suit the businesses of that time. We had restaurants, hotels and stores right on Main Street. Everything was on Main Street. The Herndon Hotel was there and the Campbell Hotel was way down the street. There was the Amador and an old, old hotel that was called the Don Bernardo. Although it was dilapidated, it was still in use.

There was a rooming house on Main and others scattered throughout the town. Then came the day of the motels. They were mostly on the west side.

The only newspaper Las Cruces had then was the *Citizen* as I can remember. There was a Spanish paper, the *Continental*. A Mr. Gildersleeve was the editor of a little bulletin and my brother, Eddie, used to work for him. Eddie was very artistic and he drew the cartoons. During election time my father used to be so embarrassed because sometimes my brother would depict somebody the way his boss would tell him. One time he drew a fat pig that was getting a big slice of the pie and it happened to be my father's friend. His friend said, "Your son drew this!" It was just a job for Eddie. I remember he used to get four dollars a week, two dollars of it in cash and two dollars in groceries. The advertiser had a grocery store and he paid for his ads in groceries. That was bartering but it was pretty good pay for a kid. My brother was an artist and sign painter for many years.

When thinking about the past, it was inevitable that the politics of that era would come up.

Way back then the people used to have arguments and fights about political candidates and issues. There were those for Hoover and those who were not. The Protestants and the Catholics, like always, were disagreeing. When Roosevelt got elected they had a saying, "El partido Democrata es el partido de los pobres" – "The Democrat is the party of the poor." It seems Doña Ana County has been Democratic most of the time, except there was an era when the Luceros were sheriffs. They were Republicans and good men. One would run, then the other one would be the deputy. They were in for years. Nobody could unseat them.

Then there was the Sam Klein era. He was mayor for twenty-five years. He wasn't about to be unseated.

Someone mentioned the WPA days. As I recall, Doña Ana County was the only county in the state that had a separate intake certification division for WPA. All the other counties had it coming out of the welfare office. It was so bad here that they had to take it away from the welfare office and have it on its own. That's where I used to work, in the intake certification department. It still didn't do much good. It was a matter of getting endorsed by the politicians. I remember they would give them a little note that would say, "Put this man or this woman to work." That's the way it was done no matter how much you fought it. The machine was very, very strong.

When I was in the administrative office of the WPA, I did intake, took dictation from investigators that went out on cases and then transcribed it. We only earned about seventy or seventy-five dollars a month.

The WPA and NYA offices and the Unemployment Service were located where the Branigan Cultural Center is now, but the building has been knocked down. NYA pay was only $17 a month, but sometimes that was all the teenagers had. I think you had to be a student to qualify for that. My sister worked with the employment office doing filing and typing. She worked one time for the, I can't remember what they called it, but they had little stations where people in costumes welcomed people. My brother worked there too when he was going to college.

The WPA was for those who needed jobs and were unskilled so they wouldn't have to be put on welfare. The men were put to work building sidewalks and construction. The women worked on sewing projects making quilts, dresses and other garments and what they sewed was given to the poor.

There was a Resettlement Administration which was set up for the farm areas. We worked with their acreage and what they were entitled to. You didn't have to qualify for that — just have your political endorsement. That office was at the college but it was moved to Amarillo, Texas. Some of the workers got assigned to go over there but I choose not to move. That was a loss of jobs from this area.

There was another project for the farmers and I worked for that too. It was when the cotton farmers were allotted so many acres for cotton and they had to plow up what they had already planted if it exceeded their allotment. They would be real mad, but they would get paid for what they plowed up.

Elsie Chilton talked about the lifestyle of young married couples in the Thirties.

I married F. P. (Bill) Chilton in August 1936. He was going to college here and working as a service station attendant in the Rogers and Moon Garage. I had a simple wedding at the old St. Genevieve's Church downtown. At that time there were very few big weddings with all the attire and the bridesmaids and everything because there was not that kind of money. They didn't have the shops in Las Cruces where you could buy wedding gowns and other formal dresses. They had to be made or ordered, or you could go to El Paso or Juarez to buy them, so most of the weddings were small and informal.

There were very few apartments of any consequence. There were boarding houses and the Valencia Courts, owned by my uncle and aunt. They were about the best at that time. They rented for the tremendous sum of $45 a month. Those who rented those apartments were college professors—Dr. Marion Hardman [Professor of English at New Mexico A & M, now New Mexico State University] lived there, and others who could afford it. There were only six or eight of those. It was real nice, but I think it is boarded up now. There were other apartments around town but we rented in what is now the Downtown Mall. They were called the Gonzales Apartments. They weren't much to be desired but they were close to where we were working and it was all we could afford. We paid nine dollars a month, all utilities paid, outdoor toilets and we had a light bulb right in the middle of the room. We pulled a chain to turn on the light. The apartment wasn't meant for ironing, and when I was caught doing some ironing, the rent was raised fifty cents a month, which irritated us. There weren't very many places like that. We had no children, and didn't stay there much. She was very choosy about who she rented to. Later on that's where Dr. Daviet's office was, on the same block near Dr. McBride's hospital. We decided to build our own house and moved out.

American Red Cross activities, early hospital facilities, as well as epidemics and death among the children were recalled by Elsie Chilton.

During the war I was very active in the Red Cross. Tommy Graham was a big wheel at that time and he worked with the Red Cross for many years until after the war. We used to go out and do social work. We would let people know what happened to their sons. If they were sending the son home after psychiatric treatment, we would check to see if the environment was all right for him to come home and how the family would receive him. We did all we could to lessen the blow for the family and for the veteran. We would investigate when soldiers asked for leave because of sickness or funerals. Mrs. Goddard was at the head of the Red Cross at the time I was working. She would dictate to me. I had a typewriter at home. I would write the letters and she would come in the evening and sign them and I would mail them. I would go out on investigations that she couldn't handle because she couldn't speak Spanish. Soon after that they hired a paid worker because the load became so heavy during World War II. The Red Cross was active here in World War II. I remember a lot of people—like the wives of soldiers of the First World War—used to say, "If it hadn't been for the Red Cross, I don't know what I would have done." During World War I, Mrs. Frank Frenger, Sr. was head of the Red Cross here.

We used to have lots of epidemics. Sometimes we would have three or four funerals. Families who had lost babies, would all be walking down to the San Jose Cemetery. The children would die of intestinal flu or whooping cough. Whooping cough would come around and leave them so devastated that if they got anything else after that, they just wouldn't survive. My mother said we lost a thirteen-month-old girl at that time. She first had whooping cough. In those early years there were no shots, no wonder drugs. You would just go to the druggist and he would say what to do. Now as I look back, it was almost the opposite of what we do now.

Elsie was eager to talk about the happy times, the cultural events, and the performing arts that took place in Las Cruces when she was young.

There were several places where plays and other entertainment took place. There were the Shadow Players. St. Genevieve's outdoor patio was a very popular place. It was centralized and lended itself beautifully for different events. Fr. Buchanan was very open-minded and approved of cultural things. His sister, Rosemary Buchanan, was instrumental in bringing performers to the patio there. At that time the Amador Hotel had lots of cultural things going on. Natalia Campbell, whose parents owned the Amador, taught ballet. The ballet dancers used to perform at St. Genevieve's and at the Amador Hotel. Gloria Hayner Shelley Campbell, who lives here now, was one of the dancers.

One time I went to...in Spanish they used to call them "Comareous." They were traveling troupes that would come and put on plays. We had a little theater and lots of hometown talent. At the Loretto Academy they had a hall where people with talent could perform. I used to tap dance. Sometimes I got paid, like when I danced for the Farm Bureau meetings. Other times it was volunteer.

We used to go to the Mesilla Dam for picnics, carnivals and concessions. Can you imagine, we used to swim in the river! At Pioneer Park there were a few things going on—not too much.

In the Twenties, when my brothers were growing up, there used to be a drug store and ice cream parlor with a player piano. It was called the "Happy Hour" or the "Elite." High school kids used to hang out there. I was too young to go there.

Lack of money didn't seem to stop us from having a good time. We didn't lament the fact that we didn't have this or couldn't go here or there because heretofore we didn't have that kind of a life. It might have slowed us down some. Perhaps, we could have gotten into more trouble if we had more money or more things. The way it was sort of held the reins. I remember my teenage and growing up years as being happy years. I didn't feel underprivileged. We took what came in stride. I think people who lost money were the same. For young people between thirteen and seventeen, that is a time when school and church, girl and boy friends are so important to them. I don't think we suffered too much.

It seems recessions are felt by more people now because big business comes in and takes over. Companies go bankrupt, jobs are lost, banks suffer and people who have been affluent have difficulties we never dreamed about during the earlier depressions. Times are just different. Now we know what is going on all over the world. Then we worried about our own little area. We went through it without hurting a great deal because it was nothing new for us. I wouldn't want to go through it again!

~~~~~~

Elsie's mother, Guadalupe Triviz Chavez, was one hundred years old when she died in 1983.
~~~~~~

~~~~~~

Elsie Chavez Chilton died June 6, 1990. She is buried in the Masonic Cemetery, Las Cruces, near her father and mother. Her husband, F. P. (Bill) Chilton and eight children survive her.

~~~~~~

Sally Parnell Durio

LOUISIANA LADY AND THE DESERT FLOODS

Sally Parnell Durio

Sally Parnell Durio was a patient in a nursing home when I visited with her in June, 1980. Sitting in a reclining chair, with her swollen feet propped by pillows, she moved her heavy body restlessly as she talked. When she started to recall childhood scenes it seemed a chore, not a pleasant experience.

I don't remember where my parents were born. It's been a long time.... I was born in Caddo Parish, Louisiana in 1889, delivered in our home by a country doctor, not a midwife. We lived in a rural area in a great big two-story house up on a hill with cedar trees all around it. I think about it often.

I was the sixth daughter. My mother had ten children, seven girls and three boys.

It got cold in that part of Louisiana. We had an old stove in the school and we used to print our shoes—you know, burn your shoes from the heat of the stove. It got plenty cold there and we had bad storms. They'd be so bad we'd think we'd have to leave the home. But we were lucky we never had any damage done. We didn't have cyclone cellars, we just stayed inside the house.

Mrs. Durio seemed to become more at ease as she continued and began to remember stories about her school days, their large family and the struggle her parents had to raise their children.

We sure had some funny kids in school. You studied history and when you were through with that, you felt you had finished with it. It was the same way with grammar and all those kinds of things in the little country school. When we moved to

Shreveport, everything was different. In Shreveport we had grades and different teachers for the grades. I started in the seventh grade in Shreveport and finished my high school there.

When we moved to Shreveport my parents weren't young any more. You know raising ten kids was a hard job. By then my dad just did odd jobs, what he felt like doing. My mother never worked outside our home.

We were Presbyterians and belonged to the church. It was different in those days. We went to church and that was it. Went to Sunday School and that was it. But now, you know how the churches do. There's somethin' goin' on *all* the time. When the door opens, there is somebody there to put on somethin'.

Sally Durio finally smiled as she thought about her youth and the fun they had.

Sometimes they called me a tomboy because I liked to climb trees. When we were in the country school we climbed sweet-gum trees.

We had a good time. They would have dances at the school house and there was a place close by where we used to go—Branch, Louisiana. I believe it is still there. When they had a big dance my mama would take the whole family—all the children. Of course, I'd go too. Those were my dancin' days.

I loved dances and parties. I think we had more fun then than they do now. I never square danced much but we used to dance the fox-trot, the two-step and the waltz. A country band furnished the music. I had a brother-in-law that played the piano and played anything you could pick up. They'd just get together, some of the fellows, and form a band and have a dance and the people would go.

I recall the night I got married, the boy that drove the taxi to the depot was a boy I used to dance with when we were kids. We were the only two kids in that bunch that danced together all the time. I was thirteen or fourteen then. I think it was a whole lot better in many ways than it is now.

Sally Durio began to talk about her life before she was married. She didn't seem to want to discuss relationships or relate discussions with her mother and other family members.

Durio

In my younger days, when I was growin' up, we'd just meet at picnics and barbecues and those kind of things. I just don't know how to express it but all the old women would get together and talk.

I don't think they talked about the women who were working on getting the vote for women. There wasn't anything about it in those days. It was a long time before that started. Women might have been better off if they had left that "lib" alone. None of my sisters or my mother was involved in woman suffrage. No, not at all. Nothing like that concerned them.

I do remember when I first voted. It was in El Paso, Texas. We had just moved there and I was scared to death. Didn't know how, didn't know what to do. I guessed at it. Maybe, it didn't count.

My husband was with me. He thought women voting was all right. I asked him about how to vote but he didn't know much more about it than I did. We didn't know anybody in El Paso. We just had to guess at it.

Sally began to talk about her sisters and then about her husband's background and how they met. She was matter-of-fact, and seemed to have forgotten any romantic incidents.

Two of my sisters taught school. But I didn't want to teach. I worked in a department store. Worked from eight in the morning to six at night six days a week. I was paid $9 a week. That was in 1910. Then I got married when I was 22.

My sister was married to a fireman in Shreveport. He got a friend that he had grown up with to come to Shreveport to take a job with the fire department. His name was Rudolph Alexander Durio. That's how it started. In a year or two, why we got married. It was 1912.

It was just a home wedding. We had a Baptist minister. A friend of ours was my maid of honor and a friend of my husband's stood up with us. It was a little family wedding. Some of my girl friends that worked with me at the store were there. It was that kind of wedding. Didn't have a bridal shower but they did throw rice after the wedding.

My husband spoke French. He never spoke English until he started school. He was from the southern part of Louisiana and I lived in the north. He became ill with tuberculosis and that's why we moved to the Southwest, where it was high and dry.

Main Street in Las Cruces, New Mexico as it looked in the 1920s and 1930s. The Durio Borderland Garage and Buick dealership were further along this street. (Photo courtesy of the Jim M. Flanagan Collection. Rio Grande Historical Collections, New Mexico State University Library.)

Durio

Sally Durio was physically unable to continue talking. Her interview was left unfinished until her son, Jack Durio told me about the experiences of his family when the Southwest was young and undeveloped. Sally Parnell Durio died December 8, 1980.

Her son, Jack N. Durio, Captain USN (Ret) lives in Las Cruces. He provided additional information about his mother so her story could be included in this collection.

My father, Rudolph Alexander Durio, came to the Southwest about 1914. He was sick with tuberculosis and came out to die. Mother stayed in Louisiana, realizing she might be left alone to raise my brother, Rudolph A., Jr.

One of my father's first actions was to go up the side of the [Organ] mountains where he bought a horse from Ollie Isaacks. The Isaacks family was one of the early settlers in Soledad Canyon. Later I married his daughter. My father started riding around the hills on horseback while the rest of the patients lay on their backs in bed waiting to die. He lasted forty-two years after that.

After dad had been in this area about a year or so my mother and brother joined him in El Paso, Texas, where they lived for three years. Their next move was to Las Cruces, New Mexico where they lived for two or three years. My sister was born here on Melendres Street. Then when she was two years old they moved back to El Paso. My dad worked for the Watkins Motor Company. He drove a Buick race car for Sam Watkins in the big El Paso-to-Phoenix automobile race they held in 1919. He came in second place. I don't remember what the speed was, but it took them about three days to complete the race. They stopped overnight a couple of times. Mother thought Dad's racing was quite exciting. She and her friends would watch as they drove by.

I was born in El Paso at the old Masonic Hospital at Five Points on June 18, 1921. We moved back to Las Cruces when I was two years old. We lived down by the old depot for a while and then moved to what used to be out in the country. It was known as the old Swank Place at that time, an adobe house out on Boutz Road. I remember we didn't have electricity. We used carbide gas lights in the house. When I was five years old my parents bought the house on south Miranda Street and my mother lived there until she moved into the nursing home just before she passed away.

My dad ran the Borderland Garage on Main Street in 1923 when they moved back from El Paso. It was the Buick dealership, but he lost that during the Depression years. After that he bought the ranch at Winston, New Mexico where we lived for about three years.

In 1936, while we lived on the ranch at Winston, I recall how my mother had to use an old wood-burning range for cooking, and that was our heat also. She adapted well to cooking on that old cast-iron range and living in a two-room house. It certainly wasn't easy for her.

I recall an exciting, but frightening, time when we lived on the ranch. We had one of those rare New Mexico floods. My parents lived in a small, wooden two-room house at the time because the main ranch house had burned down. I lived next door in another little house. It must have rained about six or eight inches in a couple of hours. The creek bed we lived on was called Poverty Creek. During the flood, water ran from our front porch all the way across to the other side of the canyon. It must have been a distance of one hundred yards where water was running solid. A dam up behind the house broke and the water came right down through the back of the house. I remember we ran out on the front porch and watched the water coming from the back door through the front door. I can still see my dad's slippers as they floated out through the front door.

When the rain finally subsided and the water quit running, we had to get in there with shovels and scoop the mud off the rug and get the place cleaned up so we could live there again. We had no other place to stay. Mother was a real trooper through it all. After we got the big mess out of the house, she had to salvage what household things and clothing she could. She survived the flood, as well as other tough times as a rancher's wife.

In 1936, after we moved back to Las Cruces, we experienced another flood. We had been on a fishing trip up on the Gila River. We came back the day after the big rain, our house on Miranda Street was on a low spot and the water drained to that corner of Amador and Miranda. The water was up as far as the front door. Our neighbors told us that the day before, every time a car would go by, the water had actually been lapping up on the front porch. They said if it looked like it was going to get in the house they were going to break in the house and try to salvage what they could—furniture and other things.

Fortunately, it didn't get into the house that time and mother was grateful for that.

When I was a kid on Miranda Street, Sheriff Pat Garrett's, wife lived over on Reymond. She was an old lady and lived with the Montgomery family. One of the Garrett's daughters married a Montgomery. I knew the Montgomery family but all the Garretts were gone by then, except Mrs. Garrett.

My mother and dad had a good relationship. I can never remember hearing them actually quarreling. They depended on each other. My mother took care of the family mostly and when something came up that required my father's attention, he was there for her.

Mother was closest to two of her six sisters. They both lived in Shreveport. Her sister Florence was married to the fireman there. Florence's husband, who was my father's friend, was the chief of the fire department in Shreveport for more than twenty years.

When I was young I visited in Shreveport a couple of times. After I was in the Navy my folks used to go back but they felt that the Southwest was home. Mother even lost her Southern accent. I don't ever remember her speaking with one.

My father was 69 when he died and mother lived alone after that until her death in 1980. She had depended on my father for financial matters but she got along all right. My brother and sister were close by to help her and she had a Mexican girl who lived with her. That lady from Louisiana certainly was a survivor!

~~~~~~

Sally Parnell Durio is buried beside her husband, Rudolph, in the Masonic Cemetery In Las Cruces.

~~~~~~

How Sally Durio felt about many things in her life, we will never know. It is a loss, but hopefully it will alert families to listen to the stories of the elderly before it is too late.

Maude Tully Guthrie

BIOLOGY AND BLOOMERS

Maude Tully Guthrie

*In January 1983, when I talked to Maude Tully Guthrie, she re-
called how she came to Las Cruces, New Mexico from Colorado
to teach at the New Mexico College of Agriculture & Mechanic
Arts. After sixty-five years of living in a community on the desert,
she looked back in time and remembered what life was like for a
young woman beginning a teaching career at what was sometimes
referred to as a "cow college."*

I received my master's degree in Biology at the University of
Colorado in 1926. Shortly after that I came to New Mexico. I
knew when I took the position at the college here that I would
be teaching biology and physical education. Dr. Kent, who was
president of the college then, seemed to feel it was necessary to
start some kind of physical education program for women. I did
initiate that and later it developed into what they have now.
The college had a women's basketball team and they won
several tournaments in 1903-05. At that time, women wore full
knee-length skirts and black stockings. By the time I started
teaching, the girls' wore black bloomers, instead of skirts, and
middy blouses. However, the dress code was very strict. The
dean of women, Mrs. Hayes, told me to be sure the girls wore
black stockings that would connect with the bloomer on the leg.
No bare leg was to show! She also said to be sure that the girls
wore coats over their uniforms on their way to the tennis courts.
She didn't want any immodest appearance of the girls as they
walked about the campus. I began teaching classes in tennis,
basketball, and archery. During the winter when it was too cold
to be outside I taught what was known then as calisthenics.

*New Mexico College of A & MA Girls Basketball
Team - 1902-03.
(Courtesy of Hobson-Huntsinger University
Archives, New Mexico State University Library)*

When I came here to the Biology Department I was surprised to find two valuable collections in the department. They were plant collections made by Wooten and Stanley—The Flora of New Mexico. There was also, the insect collection of Dr. Allison Cockrell, who had come to the college to teach entomology and I presume, related biology subjects. He gave his insect collection to the biology department when he left. Both are extremely valuable. Dr. Cockrell came from England to New Mexico and was a contemporary of many famous English professors. He had tuberculosis and came to New Mexico, like so many others, for a cure. From here he went to the University of Colorado and he was my major professor there.

The women lived in McFie Hall on campus. It was later taken over by some group from the agricultural department. I think that was the only facility available for women and also housed the dining room for all students. Students had to walk down there to get their meals. Kent Hall, the men's dormitory wasn't constructed at that time and I don't know just where the men lived. There was a house mother at McFie Hall who was also in charge of the facility. I lived in a room of a house that belonged to Dr. Kent, who was president of the college. At that time Albert and Jennie Curry lived there and rented the room to me. I lived there for three years.

I used to eat at the Blazer Boarding House, which later became the Jolly Boarding House. Henry Gustafson, whose father had the dairy here at that time, told me his father used to sell milk, butter, and eggs to the boarding house.

Mrs. Guthrie talked about women professors on the faculty at the college, and their place in society and politics in the Twenties and Thirties.

Actually, I was the only woman faculty member in Arts and Sciences. I was included in meetings and everything.

During those early years, I taught most of the agriculture students who were taking biology. I knew them better than the other students on campus. The Home Economics girls all took biology. I remember a story about one student that demonstrates how bartering helped him get into college to study agriculture. A family from Alamogordo arrived on campus with their son and a load of apples. They got to the administration building and said they wanted to get their son into college.

They had no money but they had a truckload of apples. Dr. Kent arranged for them to have the apples sold or he got them sold somehow and the son was admitted to college. The apples paid for his tuition.

Chaperoning dances was another one of her duties as a professor. At the dances we had the liquor problem to contend with. It was during prohibition. We had very nice dances. The girls wore formal dresses and usually had corsages and had program dances and got their programs filled out. They were always well-chaperoned by two or three couples. They served punch, sandwiches and cookies. They were all formal dances except the Ag Ball which, at that time, was held in the Ag barn. I do recall at one of the Ag Balls, Dr. Kent reached over to pet a very fine animal. The animal turned his head and broke Dr. Kent's arm.

~~~~~~~

Maude Guthrie, in her humble way, briefly covered the problems of a woman professor teaching in the Southwest. She did survive more than thirty-four years of teaching and established an excellent reputation for other women who followed her at the university. As a career woman she was a pioneer. She combined being a wife, the mother of two sons, a homemaker and an active member of several organizations. She retired in 1968, but not without recognition for her years of teaching.

In 1958 she received the Woman of Achievement Award given by the New Mexico A&M Associated Women Students.

On May 31, 1984 she was awarded the Regents' Medal which reads:

> *Because she diligently pursued a career devoted to teaching students how to learn and because many former students claim that her teaching was responsible for their success, the Regents of NMSU hereby award this medal.*

On April 2, 1987, in recognition of high scholarship, leadership and service, she was initiated into the Mu Beta Sorority.
~~~~~~~

Guthrie

~~~~~~

Maude Tully Guthrie, and her husband, G. L. Guthrie, Dean Emeritus, Business Administration and Economics, and Professor Emeritus of New Mexico State University, live in Mesilla Park, New Mexico.

~~~~~~

Ethel Loudermilk Heinzman

ℱIRSTS IN THE THIRTIES

Ethel Loudermilk Heinzman

Ethel Loudermilk Heinzman was interviewed in February, 1983 at her home in Mesilla Park, New Mexico. Arthritis had restricted her physical activities for many years. However, she readily recalled the years after 1926—living in the Southwest as the young wife of Walter Heinzman, Professor of Mathematics at the New Mexico College of Agriculculture & Mechanic Arts.

In May 1930, I got my degree from New Mexico College of Agriculture & Mechanic Arts. I was the first married woman to graduate as a full-time student. There were four other women who were going part-time. One was Captain James H. Howes' wife. He was the ROTC director. Mrs. Butts, the Presbyterian minister's wife, Percy Baldwin's [Dean of the School of General Sciences and Professor of History] wife, and Ellen Berry were in school at that time, but I was the first one to graduate.

The year I graduated there were six girls in a Home Economics class. As part of our household management course we were required to study and care for children of nursery school age; so we started a little nursery on campus. We would go and get the children and let them play in the sand box we built out in front of Hadley Hall. We would tell them stories and keep them entertained. I can't remember the names of all the children but there were Emily Thomas, Joan Hamiel, her mother Flora Hamiel was secretary to the president of the college; Penelope Coffee, Nancy Hollinger, and John Charles Kirby. That was the beginning of the nursery program on campus. About fifteen years later, when Education and Psychology were in one department, the actual nursery school was started as part of that department. They hired someone to run the nursery school and it grew and became an important program at the university. Our small class project in the Thirties was the first nursery.

Believe me I was pretty busy keeping house and going to school. One thing that I was especially proud of happened in the spring of '28. They wanted a swimming pool on campus. Some of us girls, along with the coach, stayed up a good bit of one night making a float that looked like a swimming pool. We put a sign on it that we wanted a pool. I went uptown the next day and got some bathing suits for children of different ages starting with our preacher's baby who was two years old. I got sizes right on up to adults so they could wear them when they rode on the float at the KKK Parade. [Note: See page 63 for additional information about the KKK.]

The Kollege Kactus Karnival [KKK] Parade was the annual May Day Festival that had been held on campus since 1902. For many years it was handled by the student body, but in 1920 the KKK group took it over.

We got the swimming pool, but we had to help build it. The boys did the digging and a lot of the work. The girls made sandwiches and cookies and lemonade and served them while the boys were doing the digging. I expect they had a contractor do the cement work, but I don't remember how much it finally cost. It was the first swimming pool on campus and it was used for many years until they built another pool.

President Kent was a wonderful man. He was very considerate of his students. He allowed me to skip chapel at eleven o'clock in the morning so I could go home and get dinner for my husband. I was given a discount on my tuition for that class I didn't take. President Kent was very good about everything—a very reasonable man.

Walter and I were often asked to be chaperones at dances and different affairs. In the spring of 1928 my brother came to visit us. We lived in what we called the doll house, a small home Lillo Holley concocted for us, next door to the Hauter's. One time, Harry Kent, Jr. came over and said the students couldn't go on their senior fling out to Dripping Springs unless they had a chaperone. I said my brother was here visiting us and young Kent said to take him along. We went. It was about fifteen miles from Las Cruces. We didn't have a car so we rode on the mattress truck. The Dripping Springs Hotel was owned by Dr. Sexton. At one time he used the old hotel for a

Wilson Hall, the Ag Building during the 1920s and 1930s. Some Home Economic classes were held in this building. The building burned in September 1937. (Photo courtesy of Evelyn R. Stevens Estate.)

tuberculosis sanitarium but it was closed that year so that's why the students had to haul the mattresses so they would have something to sleep on. In those days they had a check point you went through before you entered the Dripping Springs resort area.

The girls put their mattresses on the porch of Dr. Sexton's hotel. The boys put theirs on the roof of a shed outside. That's the way we slept that night. I'm sure we didn't do a very good job chaperoning because there were couples and they spread here and there. But, we were there. We did some climbing that weekend, but not much. My brother helped the cook because he didn't want to climb. They treated the chaperones well in those days. We were glad to go because we didn't have a car to get there ourselves.

We didn't have a car until 1935. When we were first married and Walter was teaching at the college, we would catch a ride to town [Las Cruces] or walk to the Pritchard Grocery Store in Mesilla Park.

This is how we got that first car. Our son, Homer, was born January 11, 1935, and I was still in the hospital. Walter came up to see me. Afterward, he went to the movie at the Rio Grande Theater where they had a drawing once a month. That was the night they drew for the winning ticket. And my husband had it! He won a new car. We planned to go back to Illinois that year so Walter could get his master's degree. It was sure nice to have that new car to drive. It helped us out a lot because we had to borrow money for living and tuition that year.

When we came back to Las Cruces after Walter got his master's degree, the United States was right in the middle of the Depression. The college and all the valley had financial problems. Faculty salaries were low and because there was a shortage of university funds they had trouble paying the professors. There was controversy on the Board of Regents because of political issues.

For a while Walter quit teaching and worked with the Civilian Conservation Corps as an officer. The CCC was a Federal agency set up in 1933 for the purpose of establishing a program for the conservation of the natural resources of the country and to provide work and training for unemployed young men. There were problems with that program too. One time the young men at one of the camps went on strike for better food. Some of the fellows in those camps were pretty wild.

Everybody seemed to accept their fate whatever came their way. We didn't complain and did the best we could with what we had.

I didn't have much social life. I was too busy with my family and my church so I really didn't have time to talk to other women about how they felt about politics or anything else.

Walter went back to teaching at the college. We built our home in Mesilla Park in 1939 and have lived in it all these years. Life just went on after that.

~~~~~~

Shortly before her death on June 16, 1991, Ethel Loudermilk Heinzman looked through her collection of old pictures and provided the photograph used with her story. Although in pain, she didn't complain and was most gracious and cooperative. We are sorry she didn't live to see her story in print.

After her husband Walter's death in 1989, her son Lester and his wife, Eleanor, cared for Mrs. Heinzman in her home in Mesilla Park. Her other son, Homer, and her daughter, Marita Heinzman Diebel also survive her. At the time of her death, Mrs. Heinzman had seven grandchildren and eight great-grandchildren.

~~~~~~

The first May Day celebration at State College (New Mexico A & M), was held in 1902. In 1920 the students created the K.K.K. Committee to plan the May Day celebration and also assume responsibility for painting the "A" on Tortugas Mountain each fall. A popularity election was held by the students in conjunction with the May Day events and the May Queen, Greatest Aggie, Most Popular Girl, Most Popular Boy, Most Popular Faculty Member, and Fellow with the Best Line were announced and honored at the celebration. Maude Tully Guthrie was chosen Most Popular Faculty Member in 1927.

Ruth Bundy Isaacks

$\mathcal{S}$OLEDAD CANYON MEMORIES

Ruth Bundy Isaacks

*When I interviewed Ruth Bundy Isaacks in 1983 she was
eighty-five and living by herself in an apartment in Las Cruces.
The rooms were beautifully decorated with antique furniture,
Dresden china figurines and other pieces of art. Mrs. Isaacks
showed me pictures of her family—her late husband, Emitt, her
son, and two daughters, as well as her grandchildren and friends.*

*When she brought out a yellowed photograph of a log house
with the spires of the Organ Mountains in the background, the
look in her eyes and the faint smile indicated she was remember-
ing a time which was more than seventy years ago. The springs, so
precious to the ranchers, flowed cautiously down the mountainside
and meandered through the quiet of Soledad Canyon. There were
no guns firing then or sounds of missiles hissing over the Organs.
There was a small but thriving little town, Organ, where miners
and ranchers came for grub and to pick up their mail.*

*I ignored the occasional creaking of her rocking chair as Ruth
Isaacks began her reminiscing.*

I was born in Kansas in 1898. Father, mother, my sister and I
went to Oklahoma when I was three years old. I've always been
interested in history because when we were in Ft. Sill I remember seeing Geronimo. He was sitting out beside a little adobe
shack. He was just a real old Indian. I can remember him just
as plain as can be! When we lived in Oklahoma it was Indian
Territory. We lived there a few years and then my father
moved to Amarillo. He was a carpenter and worked with archi-
tects. After that he built a courthouse in Dimmitt, Texas. Then
we went to Clayton, New Mexico where my father put up
another courthouse. While in Clayton we heard so much about

Las Cruces, that instead of going back to Amarillo, my parents thought they would drop down and see Las Cruces.

Not intending to stay in Las Cruces, we got a small place to live. A very short time later my sister became quite ill. She had an advanced degree of diabetes. There was no cure for that in those days. I started school and not long after, I got scarlet fever. I think every living child in Las Cruces had it. The fever was rampant. I survived it nicely but my sister died. After burying her in Las Cruces, my people said they would never leave here. And they never did.

I married Emitt Isaacks in 1917, after I finished high school, and went to live on the ranch in Soledad Canyon. My mother-in-law knew, and I learned, what it meant to be a wife, mother and rancher back then.

Jefferson Davis Isaacks, my husband's father, came from Erath County, Texas. They landed in Weed, New Mexico in the Sacramento Mountains, in 1887. It was the coldest winter ever known in the Territory of New Mexico. When Emitt, my husband, was born, there was four feet of snow on the level. Practically all of the wildlife, the cattle and horses froze to death. The Isaacks had twenty head of cattle left that they had under a shed, along with a team and two saddle horses that were saved by the shelter. Jeff Isaacks, his wife, their three children and Mr. Isaacks' brother, Jim, lived in their covered wagon until spring. By summer they reached the Organ Mountains and the area known as South Dripping Springs. Later, the G. R. Beasley family joined the Isaacks. The Isaacks had their stock and a $20 gold piece and got by until the next year, when they bought and traded for the Soledad Canyon. There was a spring with running water. It was like an oasis in the desert. It is to this day a beautiful canyon.

The Isaacks lived in a bunk house when they first ranched. It was a long room and a lean-to. I don't know how Mother Isaacks did it, but she was a good manager. She kept her family in those three rooms. Later, they built a lovely rock house. On Sunday morning they would hitch up the surrey—it was more of a hack—and they would be the first ones at the Methodist Church in Las Cruces for Sunday School.

Opposite page: (Top) Jefferson Isaacks family cabin in Soledad Canyon. (Bottom) Horse-drawn wagon coming from Soledad Canyon. (Photo courtesy of Rio Grande Historical Collections, New Mexico State University.)

When Emitt and I established our home, it was on the south side of the mountain in Soledad Canyon. When I was first married I was so lonely on the ranch I would sit down and cry. The only cure for loneliness was to work. And I worked a lot. People used to say I worked harder than any woman that ever lived.

There were good times too. I remember many tales of courage and bravery. My father-in-law was the best storyteller. But, it seems like we were always fighting something.

Snakes in the canyon were frightening. Jefferson Isaacks said when my husband Emitt was eight months old and just beginning to crawl, Mother Isaacks put him down on the ground. All of a sudden she saw him start to go after something and there was the biggest coiled rattlesnake ready to strike. Emitt's mother grabbed him and Father Isaacks shot the snake. That may have been when Emitt's fear of rattlesnakes started.

One time I wanted something in a small back room where we stored things. Emitt and I went up there and I was talking away when all of a sudden my husband grabbed me and pushed me out the door. I looked at him. He always had a deep sunburn but he was white. He said, "Ruth, you had your foot against the biggest rattlesnake I ever saw." I told him I wanted to see it but he wanted me to go back to the house so he could kill it. I never did see my big snake!

They would den up around the ranch. You couldn't walk to the corral and back and not see a rattler to save your life. I knew a lot of people who were bitten. Two were bitten on the heel and it didn't hurt to speak of. I hated those snakes! Actually, they are trying to get away as much as you are, but I never let them get away. I took the hoe and chopped their heads off. Once I asked Emitt if he was ever afraid of anything. I have never seen a person disturb him. He said, "Yes, if a rattlesnake rattled and I couldn't see it."

There were times when there were shaky feelings between the Isaacks and Beasley families. It was generally over water. One time, it was in the summer, Emitt Isaacks and two of his ranch hands rode over to the Beasley land at the mouth of the Soledad Canyon. They were going to look over the water supply, which was a stream right in the middle of the canyon. It was beautiful, clear, running water. They were met by two of the Beasley women, daughters of the ranch owner. We had to go across their land to get to our water. The Beasley women said they couldn't go through. My husband just sat there on his Appaloosa horse and said, "Well, get your Gatling and get posted because I'm comin' through tomorrow!"

I stayed home that day, not knowing who would kill who. They got to the mouth of the canyon and the two women were there. My husband had his gun loaded ready to shoot. It seemed like Emitt Isaacks wasn't afraid of the devil himself! The cowboys told me he said, "Pull the trigger if you have the nerve!" He just sat on his horse and smiled. The women began to cry and put their guns down. Mother Beasley said they [the men] could fight and argue all they wanted to but she and Mother Isaacks had a friendship between them that was forever. There were so few women in Soledad Canyon they needed each other.

We had Indian scares, too. Mother Isaacks told me about a time when she was very frightened. Jefferson Isaacks and his brother were going on a trip away from the ranch to help another rancher and would be gone a couple of nights. She heard them talking before they left. Her husband said, "I don't like the looks of that track I saw out there." That meant there were Indians around. In the middle of the night, she heard a noise outside. It rattled and rattled and then quit. Then it started again. She could tell by the sound that it was about where a wagon had been left in the yard near the ranch house. She was afraid to get up and see. Finally, she couldn't stand it any longer. She got up, pulled back the curtains and looked out. She saw a bucket of water in the wagon and a cow was trying to get a drink out of it!

But there were Indians in Soledad Canyon. There were markings on the walls of the cuevas [caves]. When you walked into the caves you could see that a great many fires had been built in them.

There is always something for a ranch woman to do. When it came to taking care of the fresh meat, the cowboys would always get off without doing it. You hung the meat up at night and it got chilled. Then early in the morning you would take it down and wrap it, first in some soft material, and then wrap it heavily in more material to keep the cold in. Those cowboys would be gone and I would have to wrap the meat. Being a ranch woman was not an easy life at all!

Another task I had to do would be to feed the heifers. They would come in at noon throughout the year. One by one you had to feed them. Every time I would feel bad years later, I would say, "That's from carrying those feed buckets."

My husband used to tell the story about how, when a herd of cattle was grazing with calves and there was a water hole—sometimes miles away—and the cows would walk in to get a drink, they would leave the baby calves, generally up against some tall weeds, bed them down, and one cow would stay and stand guard. I have seen a cow standing guard many times. Emitt said he thought they took turns standing guard.

I believed him when he told me about cattle because he was the best cowboy. People always said that he was. He wasn't proud, but anyone who worked cattle with him said he was just a natural. You have to be born to it. And he certainly was. Jeff Isaacks also said that Emitt wasn't very old when he saw that he had a cowboy. When he was little, he could recognize a horse, or even a cow, that he had seen a year or two before.

My father-in-law told a story about when Emitt was just a little boy. He said they had a spotted cow that had a spotted calf. The calf came up missing. They [the Isaacks] were good friends of a rancher up on this side of the mountain. The ranchers always stopped by. If they came by at noon, we fed them. So Emitt and his father stopped there one day and went into their ranch house. In those days they put rawhide on the chair seats. When my father-in-law saw the chairs, he thought, I hope Emitt doesn't see it. But he did! He said, "Papa, Papa, look! There's old Spot's calf." My father-in-law always said he didn't object to his neighbors eating his beef but he didn't like for them to butcher them and sell them.

There was cattle rustling in those days. Jeff Isaacks said some ranchers would take a brand and change it a certain way and pretty soon they were running a brand of their own. The Isaacks bought the Riley's cattle when they bought their land. But Jeff Isaacks liked sheep and kept them on the home ranch. This caused quarreling with the cattle growers. They didn't like the sheep because cattle won't graze where sheep have been.

The Isaacks had an old Mexican sheepherder. He herded the sheep and took care of them, but finally they had to sell the sheep. They would shear the sheep and take the wool to El Paso and sell it and buy supplies. They would stay at a campground. They took their own bedrolls and cooked on a little campfire there at the campground. It took a week for them to make the trip, buy the supplies, and come back.

A good ranch woman works in every area. It was my job when they were branding to weigh the cattle. The buyer would take the weight and I would take the weight and then when it was over, we had to figure what each person had coming. There would be my father-in-law's and the four boys' brands and maybe one or two neighbors'. Each one of those brands would be selling so many head of cattle. We had to keep the number and the weight of each animal. Before the buyer left you had to figure everything out. Along with that, I had to cook the meals. It wasn't no short distance from the house to the weighing pens. But I managed to do it. I walked.

One time I went with the herd. We shipped at Leasburg Dam, driving the cattle from Soledad. There were shipping pens at Leasburg. We stayed all night at my brother-in-law's.

When we worked the cattle I would get up at two a.m. It never bothered me. I could get up anytime after two. I never did know why the men got up so early, because they would sit there and drink coffee 'till daylight. Sometimes they would play penny-ante until midnight and then get up around four in the morning. I always did think that cowboys liked to make life hard for themselves. They didn't try to make it easy. They were a tough bunch.

Those cowboys! I recall a story about when they were hiring a cowboy at a neighbor's ranch. It was when the going wage for a cowhand was a dollar a day. The cowboy asked, "How much do you pay?" The rancher said, "Forty dollars a month." The cowhand said, "That goes into fractions...just make it a dollar a day."

The cowboys would work two or three months and get paid all at once. Then they would go to town, get a shave, a haircut and a bath. All that for about seventy-five cents. Maybe they would buy some Levis and shirts. They would spend all their money overnight. They would come back to the ranch and work another two or three months. But they were happy!

I liked cattle but I never liked horses. I didn't learn to ride until my husband gave me a saddle and a pretty little horse when we were first married, but then the children came along so fast that I never had the opportunity to ride much. I never was a good rider, but I would ride the range. It didn't matter. One time I got thrown and Emitt came and helped me up and picked out some of the cactus and said, "I think you better walk back to the ranch."

It made me so mad, I said, "No. I'm not going to walk one step of the way back to the ranch." I got back on the horse and went for the full day's ride.

Mrs. Isaacks stopped rocking as if time had moved forward and her thoughts were about another period in her life. She sipped her soft drink and resumed talking.

The Depression struck us just like that in 1929! We were left without any money. No one had anything. We appreciated what we did have. We used to scrounge around to get a nickel to buy a coke.

We hadn't even pulled out of the depression in the Thirties when we had a drought. It rained real hard in June of 1933, but I don't think it rained any more until 1935. We didn't market an animal in '34. My husband had to go to work for the government in a screw worm control thing. Screw worms were very detrimental to the cattle.

I had to work the cattle. One of my daughters was a natural but she was too young and the man we had working for us wasn't too knowledgeable, so I had to ride with them. Emitt would come home on the weekend and tell me what we needed to do the next week. The children hated for me to ride because there was no meal ready and they had to help, but it was a necessity.

At the start of the third or fourth drought, we had around 800 cattle with our own brand. I don't think we came out with any more than 200. What the government did is you would send for their team of killers and they would come and shoot the cow that was down, dying. If they killed her, they paid you. I believe it was $8.00, and $4.00 for a calf and $12.00 for a bull. I may be a little mistaken, but that's about what it was. It was a little money, even at that. A story was that one rancher killed more cattle than was on the Dona Ana County tax rolls. They hadn't kept a very good tally. I know we lost several hundred head ourselves. We grew back another herd in time. Then the Taylor Grazing Act[1] came into effect and they told us how

---

[1] The Taylor Grazing Act was created in 1934 to authorize the Taylor Grazing Service, now called the Bureau of Land Management. This agency administers grazing rights on public domain lands.

many we could run. We were over-grazing terribly. I always resented the fact that the government had to tell us what we should have had sense enough to have known. We had built greater herds than the country would carry. Now they tell you how many you can put on.

When the children got older we came to town [Las Cruces] and built a house so they could go to school there. I did a great deal of work for the Methodist Church on the conference level and traveled quite a bit. We would give church suppers, sometimes enchilada. Our luncheon was twenty-five cents a plate. We had come-as-you-are parties and we started rummage sales. The sales helped in two ways—it helped people who weren't able to buy new and we made some money. In a good many instances we would give away a pair of shoes or we would buy them ourselves and give them to someone who needed them badly. The Women's Society did all the work. It would cost $1.50 to get someone to wash the dishes so we washed them ourselves. We furnished everything somehow. It was hard, but we ended up with $10,000 for an addition to the church. I think that was in 1947.

Emitt would stay at the ranch but then his health broke down. The doctor told me my husband had a bad ulcer condition. If I wanted him to live I had to go back to the ranch and stop him from batching, that he was not eating right. So that's what I did. We redid the house in a Mexican motif which I didn't like. A few years later I put it in antique. That was the late 1930's and I stayed until 1957,[2] when we sold the ranch.

I remember in 1935 we were in El Paso, Texas because the first kids' rodeo was being held there. Our daughter, Jean, was elected the first rodeo queen and first girl champion. That's the year Las Cruces had the big flood. The children and I lived in Las Cruces then and my husband was batching at the ranch. There was three feet of water in our house and the city closed our street. It took a long time to repair all the damage done by the flooding.

Then, during World War II the U.S. Army wanted Soledad Canyon for a bombing range. What they paid us was so very small. I wish they had arranged it so it would come back to the owner. We have a small cemetery in the canyon where one of

---

[2] Her obituary states they sold the ranch in 1952.

my husband's little sisters and two of the Beasley family are buried. It is still the most beautiful place. It is big enough for a small ranch and by far the prettiest spot in the Organ Mountains.

Dripping Springs is nearby. Years ago they had a sort of hotel and a few little houses there. We owned the cueva and had a watering place at Dripping Springs.

On the small antique table beside Ruth Isaacks' chair were several books. Every week the woman who came in to help Mrs. Isaacks took her to the library or to one of the local bookstores. Although her eyesight was not good, her lifelong interest in books and education had not faded.

Those depression years are still vivid in my memory. I was on the school board and we had a time paying the teachers. We wouldn't hire a married woman because we couldn't have two bread-winners in a family. They had to have a degree. They hadn't had to have a degree up to that time, but we put that into effect because there would be stacks of applicants and we couldn't hire them all. It was just bad. And then we couldn't pay them. When the sales tax came in it went to the schools. That eased it down. I've always been in favor of sales tax because it did bail the schools out. Mr. Conley, who was superintendent of the schools, made $185 a month. I don't remember exactly how much the other teachers got but it was less than a hundred dollars. Then we put in that they would be paid for twelve months.

Mrs. Isaacks pointed to a framed certificate on the wall. It read:

The Legislature of the State of New Mexico having learned of the death of Mr. Emitt J. Isaacks, does hereby extend its sincere heartfelt condolences and sympathy to the bereaved family and friends of the deceased. This was an assembly in the State Capitol in Santa Fe. This official expression of its' sorrow be forthwith sent to the family on behalf of the people of the state of New Mexico.

When he died they said, "There goes Mr. Democrat." He never split his ticket in his life, never wanted or ran for an office. He just worked for the party tooth and nail. I was raised a Republican. The Methodist Church was my life and the Democratic Party was his life.

She rocked more slowly in her chair and sighed.

There is just one thing that I will claim. I was a good ranch woman, wife and mother, back then.

~~~~~~

Ruth Bundy Isaacks died May 10, 1988. She was buried in the Masonic Cemetery in Las Cruces, New Mexico beside her husband Emitt. She is survived by her son Walter of Riverside, California, and daughters Jean Berger of Monticello, New Mexico and Ethel Bundy of Chama, New Mexico.

~~~~~~

Julie Cason and Albert Johnson

SHE COULDN'T CRY

Julie Cason Johnson

Julie Cason Johnson was praying with other patients at the nursing home evening devotional when I came to interview her in 1980. She sat in her wheelchair with her head bowed. At the conclusion of the service she embraced the ministers and smiled a sweet, tender smile as she thanked them. She wheeled herself into the room she shared with another patient who was sleeping.

We can talk as loud as we want, it won't wake her up. She's deaf. Can't hear a word.

I was born on a farm close to Brady, Texas. Mother was born in Arkansas but moved to Texas when she was very young. My father was born in Texas too and lived there all his life. I was born at home. Hospitals were kind of scarce eighty-nine years ago. I'm sure I was delivered by a doctor, not a midwife.

I had two brothers and three sisters. My family live to be very old. My older sister is now living in California. My oldest sister lived to be 95 and my oldest brother was 93 when he died. My youngest brother passed away last year. He was only 83. I would like to visit my sister in California but neither one of us is able to make the trip.

My family farmed. We all worked on the farm—helped pick cotton when we were young. Mother helped too and cooked and did all the housework.

My mother and I were close. You know I miss her lots even—to this day. She was always so good to us. Well, good to everybody. She was such a good-natured person. When I had problems I went to mother with them. She died at eighty-three. My father died several years before that. My baby sister died and she had two little girls. My mother raised them. They were the grandest girls you ever seen. They live in California. But they never went off and left my mama by herself. They are in their fifties now. She took care of them until they got in their teens and then when Mother got nearly blind and couldn't get around, they took care of her; better than us kids could. After Mother died, their daddy and them moved to California.

I didn't have any daughters to come to me, but I had my sons. My mother had two sisters who were living with us when they passed away. Our family always helped out each other.

We all went to school but we didn't have school then like we do now. I think it was better then. We didn't get a big education but we learned more in a short time than they do now in high school. They taught us different. We went to a country school and studied reading, writing and arithmetic. The teachers were men and women at different times. We would walk to school and take our lunch in a little bucket. If you put somethin' in a kid's lunch bucket now they'd think they were ruined. My father would sell out and move so we changed schools several times.

It wasn't until 1929, after I was married, that my husband Albert and I sold out and came to New Mexico. I lived in Texas all the time when I was a girl.

Holy pictures and a Bible were close by Julie's bed. She spoke with respect about her parents and with fondness and reverence about religious experiences in her formative years.

My mother worked a lot in the field on the farm but she never worked outside our home. She always had time for church. We went to church more then than now. My folks were good people. We used to go to the big brush arbor[1] in the summer. I was down in Texas about eight years ago and I saw one or two of the old arbors. We passed them on the road. I was with my niece. They looked so good. They were old but they brought back memories.

In the arbors they preached just like they do in the church house here. We'd have these meetings in the summer. It was so nice. I don't remember that they had music but I remember the preachin' and the church.

Bitterness crept into her voice when talking about social activities and politics. Her answers were spontaneous and to the point.

I don't remember having birthday parties, not like now, anyway. They make so much out of nothin' these days.

---

[1] Brush arbor, or camp meetings, were important religious and social events in the early days of the Southwest. Once or twice a year they gathered from miles around for several days of preaching, singing, eating and visiting. The men built a three-sided shelter of brush for the visiting preacher. During the day they participated in the worship services and in the evenings ate and visited. Families camped out in and under their wagons. Brush arbor meetings were eagerly anticipated each year.

I recall my mother, my sisters and the women relatives never thought of such a thing as women voting. I remembered when I was married my father-in-law said, "If they win, the world will go bad!" And it has. You know it has.

I wouldn't say the women caused it, but I think they did. They have taken the men's places in too many things. They throwed too many men out of work. It got to where the farmers couldn't get men to work and they just changed everything so I think that's what's the matter with us now.

When we talked about dancing and the friends of an earlier time in her life, it was apparent that the memories were happy. Grasping for contacts with that past was understandable.

We had lots of country dances and I used to go to them. I learned the other day that a man who played in the fiddlers' contest here also played where I used to go to dances in Texas. He is about my age. He had three brothers. They would take turns. Two of them would play and one would dance.

A few years ago I went to a place where fiddlers stayed when they came to the fiddlers' contest. I saw this old boy a fiddlin' and I said, "Why, I know that fellow. I used to dance with him when I was a girl!" Somebody said, "Why don't you go over there and see if he remembers you." So, I did. The room was crowded, but I got there. I said to him, "I don't guess you remember Julie Cason of Robert Lee." He said, "I remember a pretty little black-haired girl." I said, "There's been lots of water run under the bridge, since then." They called him T. Green.

There was a fiddlers' contest the other day around here and I said to a friend of mine, "You see if T. Green is there, 'cause if he is still alive, he'll be at that contest." He lives in Tempe, Arizona. He's a little older than I am. But my friend told me he wasn't there.

I remember how we used to dance in the homes. Everybody went. I started going with boys when I was about seventeen. I had other boyfriends but I never cared for none of them, except Albert. Guess I was about sixteen when we bought a farm close to where his family farmed. It was close to Robert Lee, Texas.

Albert and I went to dances and church together. We saw each other every Sunday but were in no hurry to get married. He passed away in 1952 when we were living in Truth or Consequences, New Mexico. We moved there after he couldn't farm anymore. My youngest son lives in Las Cruces now.

When my son was here from Texas he counted my grand-children and he said I have forty-eight. And I have great-grand-children and great-great-grandchildren. They gave me a surprise birthday party last December when I was eighty-nine.

We were married on Valentine's Day, February 14 in 1909. I was married at home and wore a pretty white dress. My mother was an awfully good hand to sew. She made it. It had long sleeves, and you didn't see much neck either in those days. Not many brides wore flowers in their hair. I didn't. It was such a nice wedding.

After we were married we farmed with his folks but we had a home of our own. We had five sons. The oldest was born June 3, 1910. Three were born in Texas and two in New Mexico.

Julie Johnson and her boys.

We weren't satisfied in New Mexico so we went back to Texas one year. Albert didn't like dry-land farming. But then we turned around and came back and been here ever since.

Julie Johnson's memories of events outside her own family were meager. She answered readily when I inquired about when she first voted and if she ever wanted to be other than a housewife.

Well, I never did vote but once in my life. I voted for John Kennedy and then he was killed and I said I never will vote no more. I just didn't want to vote before that. It wasn't that my husband didn't want me to. He always voted but I thought men could tend to it better.

I worked in the field on the farm. I never wanted to be a teacher, or nurse or work somewhere other than in my home. I was satisfied there. We had a good home life and we got along good. We always got along good. We was happy together.

Julie's sensitive nature was easily recognized as she continued to speak of her husband's lengthy illness and his death in 1953.

I was feeding him his supper on Christmas Day. All at once he just leaned back and I screamed. The boys heard me and when they saw their father, they called the doctor. They took me out and when the doctor came they asked him to get something to quiet me down. And you know, I haven't cried one time since. I could cry up 'til then.

About five years ago my grandson drowned. He and a big horse fell into some water near Phoenix at Glendale, Arizona. They had a diving crew from Phoenix looking for him. They liked to never found him. His poor mother and daddy had to wait. I couldn't shed a tear. I cry inside. It hurts so bad. I felt so bad I had to fly home. I couldn't ride in the car.

I've been to several funerals. It makes me feel bad that I can't cry. People look at me and they think that I don't care. But, oh Lord, they don't know what I go through. I had a nephew that was killed in El Paso. He was driving an oil truck that was in a wreck and burned up. That was the saddest funeral and I couldn't shed a tear. His sister looked at me so hard but she didn't know that I couldn't cry. It makes it hard on ya, but I just choke up in here. [She put her hand on her breast.] If I could just hollar, but I can't talk or say nothin'. It would be so much easier if I could let my grief come out. Oh Lord, yes. I wouldn't be living here if it hadn't been for that.

Before I came here I lived by myself in a little government house. Sometimes I would nearly pass out before I started my breakfast. My sons worried because they didn't want me to live alone, but I thought that was nonsense. Anyway, that's why I'm here, so they won't be worrying about me.

"I always have to take something to make me sleep," Julie said, when the nurse came into the room with her medication.

Julie wanted to talk more, but the nurse shook her head. Her other memories would have to wait for another time.

~~~~~~

Another time never came. Julie Cason Johnson died March 13, 1983. She was buried near her beloved husband, Albert F., in The Garden of Memories Cemetery in Hatch, New Mexico. L. B. Johnson, the eldest son, died in 1985. Jimmy lives in Phoenix, Arizona, Homer and the youngest son Willie live in Las Cruces, New Mexico and Donnie lives in Levelland, Texas.

~~~~~~

Genevieve Martinez Lucero

NEW YEAR'S BABY - 1906

Genevieve Martinez Lucero

Interviewing Genevieve Lucero in February 1983 was a reward-ing experience. She had a happy, optimistic outlook on life despite the many problems of her yesterdays. There are sorrows, disap-pointments, joy and courage in this scenario of a woman striving for happiness against many odds.

I was the first baby born in Las Cruces, New Mexico in 1906. My mother said they gave her lots of gifts for me. I was only two days old when my father died. Mother married again. My step-father was Jose Martinez. He had two daughters and then he and my mother had two sons so there werc fivc children in our family when I wns growing up.

We lived across the street from the old Gallagher house and the Loretto Academy in Las Cruces. The Academy had boarders who stayed there all the time and day students who went home every night. The boarders paid $35 a month. If the girls had a private room, they paid $45. Parents had to furnish sheets, towels, and stuff like that. Tuition got higher later years. But there were lots of girls that boarded. They came from dif-ferent places, back East, Mexico, all over. People used to send their children to Loretto Academy. Loretto was very well-known throughout the United States. Later years, during the Depression, it didn't seem to make any difference, they had lots of students.

My mother and father, as well as my step-father, attended Loretto, so the Sisters knew our family very well. When my mother married my step-father he had two children by a previ-ous marriage. The younger was two years old. I guess the nuns felt sorry for mother having two small children and a new baby to care for because when I was about five months old the Sisters from the Academy used to come and pick me up and I'd stay with them from nine o'clock in the morning until five in the evening. Then I started school there. The Sisters taught me how to read and write, and, of course, catechism. They even taught me fancy dancing. Sister Defrosa used to teach toe dance, ballet, tapping, and Sister Magdaline was the music teacher, but she taught us the slower dances like the waltz.

The Loretto Order of nuns ran the school. Mother Barbara was the head of everything. Sister Lilly used to take care of the library. Sister Mary Ann took care of the girls who didn't know how to speak English and taught them English. The boarders were all girls, but some boys from ages seven to twelve were day scholars.

I was usually very quiet. One time Sister Arsella took us on a picnic to the Organ Mountains. We were walking out there and had to cross a kind of ditch. Sister told me not to jump across it because it was too far for me. The girls told me to jump. They said, "You can make it!" I listened to the girls instead of the Sister, so I jumped. I hit my lips and knocked out my two front teeth. Sister got real mad at me because I didn't do what she told me to do. It was all my fault. Then she said, "You're goin' to look very beautiful, now." She got after me for that. I cried for a while. Then I started to play, but my mouth looked terrible. Later on they took me to the dentist and he gave me something for the pain. When I was about ten the doctor put two false teeth in there.

Of course, we had to be real quiet in school, not do this or that, not talk or turn around. I used to look around and see the children. Then when Sister Claudine wasn't looking, I would take out my two teeth and make faces and everybody laughed. Sister said, "Everybody has to be punished except Gen, the only one doing nothing." I put my head down. 'Course I knew it was my fault. The second time I did it, everybody got punished again except me. I thought it was no good for all the girls to be punished when it was my fault so I went to Sister. I said "I got something to tell you." She said, "No, no, go on, you're not punished." I said, "I'm the one who should be punished, not the girls, because I'm the one who made them laugh."

"But, how could you, I didn't even see you. I know you didn't."

I said, "I'm the guilty one." She said, "What did you do?" I took out my teeth and made a face. Then she laughed. I said, "See, you laughed too and you're not supposed to laugh, either." She said, "OK, I'll let them go." "Punish me," I said. She said, "No, you're honest and told me the second time you did it, so I'll let you go." So none of us was punished that time.

When my father bought a ranch in Garfield, my mother and the rest of the family went to Garfield. I was still in grade school so I stayed at the Academy.

I loved to roller skate and I was a real good skater. We had a place in back of the Academy that was all sidewalk and we skated and played tennis and basketball there. When we played those games or skated we wore white middy blouses and black satin bloomers.

Not long ago I went to a roller rink and I skated too. I fell once and then this girl said, "Oh, no, you're not going to skate any more." I said, "It's fun." But she said, "You might break your hip." I told her, "I'm not afraid about that because I won't fall that hard." But, I didn't skate any more.

The father's authority in the family during this period in history is again evident when Genevieve talked about what she wanted to do.

I had a wonderful time at the Academy. At one time I wanted to be a nun but my father wouldn't let me, so when I was in the sixth grade he took me out of the Academy. They had moved back to Las Cruces then. He didn't say why or anything so I asked my mother. She said, "You have to do what your father said." He was always considered my father because he was the only father I knew. I got angry at him because I loved to be there. Finally, I got over it. I accepted it. I thought maybe this is what God wants me to do. They told me I had to go to Central School. I went there but I didn't like it. I wasn't happy at all. I didn't go to school anymore after the seventh grade. I wanted to work and make some money.

My father used to work for Mr. May who had a big mercantile store where you could buy almost anything you might need—clothes, shoes, groceries, everything. My father had six horses he would hitch up to a covered wagon and drive to El Paso to get supplies for the store. It would take three days to go and three to come back because they had to stop and rest the horses. He would stay home a day and then take the wagon to

Genevieve and Benny Lucero with their wedding party.

Organ with supplies for the store there. That would take a day to go and a day to come back.

My first job was working in the Walker home. The Walkers had a store and I helped Mrs. Walker with her children. I wouldn't have to work on Sunday. After Mass I would go to Shank's Bakery and buy a whole bag full of sweet rolls. They cost twenty-five cents and bread was fifteen cents a loaf. The family had the bakery and they did all the baking. Everything really tasted good.

Every year at the Loretto Academy they had a kind of fair. We all made things to sell, like embroidered dresser scarves and aprons. We would walk around selling stuff from our baskets. The money we made would go to help the Sisters. We would have box lunches and the men would bid on those and then you would go eat with the man that bought your box.

I wasn't in school there anymore but I was helping at the fair. Benny Lucero got my box. I didn't want to go eat with him, but Sister Arsella made me go over and sit down. I didn't know what to say so I didn't say one word. He did all the talking. Then he asked me to dance and I fibbed, "I don't know how to dance." Sister heard me and she said, "If you don't go dance I'm going to pinch you." So I went and danced with him because Sister Arsella could really pinch.

Then Sister told us we had to go and sell some more stuff. Benny bought everything I was selling. Finally it was over and I said, "Thank God!"

We went together for four years before we got married. I was 19. It was a pretty big wedding at St. Genevieve's. I had six bridesmaids, a maid of honor and two flower girls. I wore a long white dress and a veil with a train. Fr. Buchanan was the Priest who performed the ceremony and the other Priest who had charge of the music was from Spain. I knew him because I sang in the choir at St. Genevieve's. The organ he played had to be pumped and back then we sang the Mass in Latin.

We lived in Las Cruces after we were married but my husband couldn't get a job so I had to go to work. Dr. McBride had his office and a small hospital in the back of his house that was downtown across from the library. I used to help in the hospital and in the home. Mrs. McBride—she and all in the family were very nice and they were good to me. I used to take care of Mrs. McBride's elderly mother. I would feed her, braid her hair and she was so grateful. Dr. McBride would go all over making house calls and delivering babies. I got my board and room and five dollars a month. That was before my children were born. Dr. McBride said I should try to save money and put it in the bank but I would give mine to my mother to keep.

Even after my three sons were born, I kept on working there because my husband just didn't provide for our family. My mother would take care of the boys. Sometimes Benny wouldn't be around at all and I knew he was stepping out on me so, eventually, I got a divorce. At one time I put two of my boys in the Isleta Convent in El Paso. It was hard trying to keep my family together. I worked for Dr. Sedgwick and other doctors for many years.

I learned a lot about different diseases. My second son, Tony, got meningitis when he was fifteen days old. Three doctors, including Dr. McBride and Dr. Sexton worked on him in a room in our house. They didn't want to move him. They said the treatment was an experiment but if it saved him it might save the lives of other children too. My mother said, "Go ahead and do it. If he is going to live, he will live and if he is going to die, he will die."

They laid him on the table and gave him a shot in his spine. They gave him another shot of what looked like clear water. Then they drained this yellow stuff out of my son's spine. I watched them doing it all. I was so frightened, but I wouldn't leave. After he was through the doctor said, "Don't move him. Leave him alone. I don't think he will wake up." All he had for two days was drops of water. Then the doctors said to put two drops of whiskey in a big spoon of rice water and that's all we could feed him for three days. The doctor closed the place on his back where he got the shots and he was all right. He grew up, played and went to school. Now he is married and has two children. My mother said, "Now you can use that on somebody else." We were very thankful and I was so grateful to my mother who supported me then.

There were quite a few cases of smallpox in the late 1920's and the 1930's. Some people tried to treat themselves. They would make a paste with coco and put in on their faces and bodies to stop the bad itching. It would harden and they wouldn't scratch so they didn't have any scars at all. They were supposed to be vaccinated but some were afraid of that.

Later on I got married again. The fellow's name was Charlie Sour. He used the name Letting too. I had a baby girl. That marriage didn't turn out much better than the first one. He drank a lot and died after a few years and I was left alone again with a family of growing kids to feed and educate. It didn't cost us so much to live then. I remember you could buy material for fifteen cents a yard and my mother would make dresses for me and my daughter. 'Course there was more expensive material, but we couldn't afford that.

I never had difficulty getting a job in Las Cruces, because they [employers] knew me and they would ask me if I needed a job. I worked half a day at Mr. LaPoint's printing shop. I'd fold the papers and get them ready for the street and whatever they asked me to do. I got seventy-five cents an hour. 'Course I didn't have to pay my mother for taking care of the children so I got by somehow.

During the Depression I worked on the Doña Ana County WPA Sewing Project. The sewing machines were in a big room in the courthouse and there were about twenty girls/ladies from Vado, Mesilla, Doña Ana and other places in the county who worked there from eight o'clock to five. We sewed T-shirts and jeans. Some of the ladies made buttonholes. We had to make our quota and were paid by the hour. I don't remember how much. But if we made over our quota we were paid extra.

The hardest things to sew were men's and children's blue jeans. Women didn't wear jeans at that time. You never saw a woman in jeans. The small ones were hardest to make—especially the band, the fly and all that. They were much harder than the big ones.

I worked quite a few years on the WPA. It really helped me out. The men who worked on the WPA built sidewalks. That's when we got more sidewalks and people seemed better off. The banks closing never bothered me because I didn't have any money to put in the bank. I used to give it to my mother to save it for me.

Just before World War II, things were a little better for me. I started working in the Main Cafe. I was a waitress there for a long time. I got three dollars for half a day plus tips. I used to make pretty good tips. I had special customers. The Lancasters used to eat there three times a day and Mrs. Lancaster would try to get me to serve her. One day she said, "Genevieve, I want some tea, and I mean tea." Hardly anybody ever asked for tea. So I went to Jimmie, who owned the cafe and cooked, and told him. He said, "She must be an English lady. I'll fix the

*Main Street Cafe in Las Cruces, New Mexico. A familiar
landmark for many years.*

tea for you." I brought the tea out to her that Jimmie had made. She said, "This is not tea! The water isn't even hot. Call that Jimmie over here." She really bawled Jimmie out and he got mad. I went back and boiled some water in a pan and put the tea in and took it out to her. "Who made this tea?" Mrs. Lancaster said. I told her I did and she said, "I thought so. That man doesn't know how to make tea." She still works here in Las Cruces and reminds me of that every time I see her. She's a wonderful person!

In all her reminiscing about the persons in her life, she always spoke of them with respect and never looked at the dark side of people, places and events. Her friends are forever.

~~~~~~

Genevieve Lucero lives in the old adobe home that was built for her by her father when she was first married over fifty years ago. It is just a block or so from where the Loretto Academy was located. On Sundays she attends Mass at the new St. Genevieve's Church on Espina. She enjoys life to the fullest, spends time at the Munson Senior Citizen's Center where she sings in the chorus and participates in many activities, including dancing. What she learned from the Sisters of Loretto so many years ago is still very real to her.

~~~~~~

Mary Hendricks Masters

DAYS OF SEGREGATION

AND OTHER STORIES

Mary Hendricks Masters

On a beautiful day in May 1991, Mary Hendricks Masters met me at the Munson Senior Center in Las Cruces, New Mexico for our interview. She apologized for being a little late, explaining that she was helping a friend whose husband had been hospitalized. As we talked about her childhood, her later years, and her career, it was apparent that helping everyone, including those in her own Black community, was the most vital part of her life.

I was born in Mississippi in 1916 and lived on a farm with my parents and nine siblings. I was the tenth child. Two of the children died. My father raised cotton, vegetables and corn.

My mother was not an excitable person. She seemed to be very much at ease with the family. She took things in her stride. My father was just the opposite. He was accident prone. It seems something was always happening to him so it helped that my mother was calm. Father had been hurt several times. The time I remember most vividly was when he was found near a creek where he had fallen off the wagon. He was taken to the doctor and later was brought home. That time we got the news before he came home and when he did come home he was moaning and groaning. I thought that was the end. My mother and my older brother went in the buggy, but they missed him so she wasn't at home when he got there. By the time she got there other neighbors had crowded in throughout the house.

The next morning when the doctor came he was whistling, "Let Jesus Fix It For You." Then he spoke to my mother and said, "Stella, I thought you would have been a widow by this time." My mother didn't say anything. She just wasn't excitable. I expect she held a lot of things inside, rather than expressing them outside. My father did get well after that accident and lived to have many more accidents.

I had so many sisters near my age that we played and did everything together and had lots of fun. I expect that helped me later in life. When I was teaching and living with other women teachers, I got along well, seemed to fit into the group, and was able to adjust to any situation. My brothers and sisters didn't have much time for communicating with our parents or each other because there was always work to be done.

My mother sewed. As soon as the children were old enough, those that were interested, learned to sew and made their own clothes so they could fashion them like they wanted. I started sewing when I was nine and made clothes for my doll. When I was older we girls used to walk two miles to the dressmaker and she would make a pattern of a dress if we showed her a picture of what we wanted. She charged fifteen cents and we could buy material for as low as fifteen cents a yard. Our dresses didn't cost us very much in those days.

We went to a little school that was on my father's farm until I was in the fourth grade. In 1926, Mississippi consolidated the schools and I went to the school at Lampton, which was on my grandfather's farm. My grandfather and my father more or less owned their land. They were not sharecroppers. I went through the tenth grade there. I remember the year because my brothers bought a 1926 Ford. They paid $500 for their new car.

During the time one of my older sisters was ill and I was nine, I stayed in the house and did the cooking with my sister supervising. I learned how to make bread too and even today my family and friends say my dinner rolls are special. They accuse me of having a secret recipe but I think it is just the same as any other. I still like to cook. What I learned at home I used in my home demonstration classes along with what I learned in Home Economics classes in college. I had to help out with the cooking because my mother was out in the fields with the other part of the family. My mother was a large, compact woman and very healthy. She had a good stature and handled the work outside very well. They had to chop cotton, and plant corn, peanuts and other vegetables. We always grew a good garden.

Before I came to the city to live, our social life was around the church in our little town. We did a lot of church work and that's where we met our girl and boy friends. We worked through the week and Sunday was a big day. We would walk from church to church. I had a few boy friends but when I moved, that changed things. I kept in contact with some.

At the time I was growing up, we didn't dance, and we didn't play cards. I didn't know what a card was until I went to college. I didn't do much dancing and there were no theaters because we were out in the country. I started going to movies after I left home. We did a lot of singing. But didn't have instruments like pianos and organs. We sang by the shape of the notes. We would sing the notes and then we would go back and sing the verses. This was the way we learned gospel singing.

When I was very young my father worked away from the farm. He did logging; used a team of oxen and later had mules. There were forests near where we had our farm. It was a green, lush area and most people were satisfied with their lot. At that particular time, nobody seemed to want to move out. They seemed satisfied living on the farm because the older people were reared on the farm and then their families just stayed on following what their families had done before them. They felt that was their place at that particular time but later things changed. I didn't feel like most Black women of that time. I didn't want the kind of life my mother and grandmothers had. I was eager to do more—to move on.

When Mary spoke of leaving her immediate family and going to live in a completely different environment, it was evident that the change affected the rest of her life.

When I was about fifteen or sixteen, there was a principal who came to our school and stayed one year. I was very close to the Home Economics teacher, so when she visited with our former principal she told him she thought I would be the ideal one to come and live with them. The teacher thought since I was from a big family and was a good student, it would be an opportunity for me to go on with my education. The principal's wife was a teacher too and taught in Mississippi. Their name was Dean. I asked my parents if they would let me go and live with the Deans. They said I could, so that's what I did.

While living with the Deans, I was considered a family member and I took care of my own personal needs. Later I took over some of the family duties. The Deans were Black and had no children. They usually had some young person in their home while they were employed as principal and teacher.

It wasn't emotional for me to leave my family because at that time it allowed me to pursue what I wanted—a better life for myself. I had ideals and that is why I stayed with them. My goals were set. I made the adjustment with the Deans very easily because it was something I wanted. I was living in the city, and moving from the country was a drastic change. But it really didn't affect me that much. I made friends very easily and when it was just about time for school to start I met a nice girl who lived on the same street and we went to school together. That classmate and I were together for two years.

All my education was in segregated schools. When I was in the city I was in a church school. I had no part of the religion in it. This man and his wife discussed it. She had been raised as a Catholic and he had gone to a public school. She wanted me to go to the Catholic school and he wanted me to go to the public high school. A close family friend came to visit and she had a daughter about my age. Evidently, they knew I was coming. Her daughter was going to a church school right there in Jackson, on the west side. It was called the AME School—African Methodist [Episcopal]. So that's where I went instead of the two schools the Deans had suggested. I went an entirely different route in my education. I attended the Episcopal Church with my girl friend and my classmates, but I didn't join. My father was a Baptist and my mother a Methodist. They attended those churches before I was born. Relationships with their churches are something that stick with children. After I was grown, I associated with the Methodist as well as the Baptists. I do believe families should have some religious training. At the time when kids are small you generally take them to the church of your choice. Later, when grown, I feel they should be able to make up their own mind. I don't think they should be forced into either the father's or the mother's religion.

My father died an accidental death at 59 in 1935. He was logging at the time. I was in college then. My mother died in 1948. She wasn't used to taking over, the business-type thing, but I think she was a better manager than my father. If my father had the managerial ability my mother had we would have lived a different life. Mother was a midwife and my oldest sister went around with her to do things business wise. That sister became a midwife later on. I had seven sisters that lived to be grown. My two younger sisters finished college. My sisters and myself were the first ones to go off to college. By the time they were ready to go on with their education, I was already living with the Deans in Jackson.

The couple I lived with changed jobs and taught at Alcorn College, so my senior year in high school I took my classes at the college. In 1940 I got my bachelor's degree in Home Economics – that's fifty years ago! I studied one summer at Tuskegee Institute.

After I got my degree, I taught Home Economics in Alexander High School in Mississippi. Then later I moved to Oklahoma where I worked in a one-room school for about four months. I was waiting for another job to develop. I had seven or eight pupils, everyone floated without being classified, I taught everything. The schools were still segregated in Oklahoma so all the children were Black.

All her life Mary Hendricks was aware of discrimination. To be a Black, single woman, during the years she was striving to have that better life, made everything so much harder.

These were the war years and my nephew was in the service. All my boy friends were in the war and none were killed. During those years, I became a home demonstration agent in Oklahoma. I was assistant to the agent there, who was white. The government created this War Food Production and Preservation Assistant job in place of Home Demonstration Agent. Every time I wrote my name I had to put that long title under it. That's why I remember it so well. Every week I reported to my supervisor. I didn't have a designated place to work. I just went out in the community or I drove along a country road and if I saw somebody that I thought needed help I would go in, introduce myself, offer my help for canning of what was growing in the garden or anything that they needed. At that time I did quite a bit of demonstrating how to can and preserve food.

There was some poverty there and a large number of people were moving out of Oklahoma and going to war jobs. One of the things I had to adjust to was the split school situation. In the farm area they went to school two months in the summer and the other session was in the fall. That made a difference. I dealt and worked closely with Black families only and they were very appreciative of what I did for them.

At the time I met my husband, Alfred, I was the home

demonstration agent in Idabel, Oklahoma. My county agent was one of his best friends. Alfred used to visit the office. He was an ex-Marine and *The Daily Oklahoman* put his picture in the newspaper when he was sworn in on June 1, 1942.

> Alfred Masters, 26-year old Oklahoma City Negro at 12:10 a.m. Monday, became the first Negro ever to be enlisted in Oklahoma by the United States Marines.... Masters is now a civilian employee in the Army Air Corp. He has completed four years at Langston University.

He served in Guam and overseas and had started back to school because he lacked a few credits for finishing his degree. His supervisor had advised him to come down to the lower part of the county to take a job training returning soldiers for farm work. That's what he did. That's where I worked and that's how we happened to meet. He was an agriculture major. We had a lot in common—same background and worked in the same field. He was reared by a widowed mother in Oklahoma and went to Black schools. He never knew his father.

We went together about three years before we married. It was a very easy-going relationship since we were in related fields and our interests were more or less similar. I was a career woman, very independent. I could fix a flat if I had one.

One funny thing happened when Alfred and I were going together. A former boy friend I knew in college was going to be playing baseball in Paris, Texas. He sent me a wire and at that time I was just recovering from surgery. I had been off the job for about two months. I called my friend in Hugo, to ask her if she would drive me over to Paris, which is about forty-five miles from Hugo. I was going to take the bus to Hugo and then we would drive to Paris and spend the day and see my old boy friend. How Alfred found out that I was planning on going on that trip, I don't know to this day. When I walked up to my car in the driveway, there was Alfred. I asked him why he was there and he said he decided he would take me to the bus station. So I got in his car and all of a sudden I realized he was on the highway on the road to Hugo. He wasn't going to the bus depot. I didn't know what to think but I couldn't very well jump out of the car. He didn't give me any explanation. He just let me out at my girl friend's place and left. We had a little tiff about that, but it kinda blew over because I came back the same day. He was very much outgoing when he wanted to be.

When we got married, we were both working in Oklahoma and it was at a time when the agency hired only single women. The reason for that was because they said home demonstration work was one job and taking care of your family was another one. They thought with both jobs you had too much responsibility. If there was an older woman who had raised her family, they would hire her. There were very few counties in Oklahoma who had Black women working. Things were separate. The white and black county workers had separate offices. Our offices were much smaller and our director was at Langston University, a Black school.

We got married secretly in Arkansas in 1949 by the justice of the peace. I wanted to continue to work as a single woman instead of as a married woman because I knew if I told them I was married I wouldn't be able to keep my job as a home demonstration agent. Alfred left shortly after our marriage for a job in Arizona, so we weren't living together for about a year and a half. Then he got a job in Cleveland, Ohio and I resigned.

My husband's mother lived in Las Cruces and I came to visit her before my first child was born. I met the family for the first time then. And I almost lost that baby when I was playing out at White Sands with one of my nieces. The doctor put me to bed for a week and then I went straight back to Cleveland.

In 1952, I worked in Cleveland for about six months before that baby, my first child, was born. I had three girls and two boys. The youngest boy was born in 1958. I started to work again when my youngest boy was in kindergarten. The kids kind of wanted me to work because all their friends' parents were working.

Even when Mary Masters was not on a social agency payroll she continued to help families in need. She kept reaching for higher goals and pursuing the good life, not only for herself, but for her family.

When my family was growing up in Cleveland, a most tragic thing happened that I will never forget. A little girl down the street reached up to a get a glass of something off of the fireplace. It was one of those movable fireplaces that wasn't attached. The fireplace fell over, struck and killed her. She was only two or three years old. The community people came in and cleaned up the house, which was filthy. We got everything ready for the funeral. I remember how appreciative the young family was. I mended clothes so they would have something to wear to the funeral. It was so sad.

My husband held down two jobs when the children were growing up and he was a good father. We worked together in raising our children. My friends in Cleveland all worked and they encouraged me to go back to school and get certified to teach in the schools there. I started but then I stopped when we moved to New Mexico in 1965. My children were all in school and they wanted me to go back to work. They never experienced segregated schools either in Cleveland or in New Mexico.

When I came to Las Cruces I thought this was the dirtiest place I had ever seen. I had to adjust to the dust storms and the desert climate. It was so different from where I came from. I guess I have survived it though.

Mary shared stories about some of the cases she handled during her years as a social worker. The compassion and understanding she demonstrated were a reflection of her caring and thoughtfulness for her fellow man.

I spent eighteen years and three months as a social worker for the Department of Human Services in New Mexico. I had to take the test in order to qualify for the position. When I started I was a child welfare worker. If I worked with a family, it had to be a family with children. In some situations they were not functioning as normal families. That's when I ran into difficulties.

When I worked with the agency, dealing with low-income people who were mostly welfare clients, I saw a lot of infants, children and mothers in need of better nutrition.

One experience I had was with an unwed mother who had left home. I was given the case of this girl, maybe she was sixteen. I had to take her back to her mother because that was what my supervisor advised me to do. It was a very hard task to tell this woman that her daughter was pregnant. It was a Hispanic family and I was surprised that the mother wasn't more emotional about it. They worked it out and the girl decided to keep the baby. It was talked out, but the first meeting on cases like that was always the hardest for me. And through the years, there were many similar cases but it was always depressing and emotional for everyone involved.

I also worked on adoptions. It was hard to place mixed or Black babies and find the right families for them. Some persons had specific requirements, like blue eyes and blond hair and other background information. That was where the trouble came in. There was always that grey line to be able to distinguish whether or not the family really wanted the child. If the adoption failed you would feel like it was your fault. It was a big responsibility working with adoptions.

Finding a home for older children, usually created problems. Working with the family to find out whether they really wanted a particular child was frustrating. When a family is approved for adopting a child, there is a trial period of one year before final papers are drawn up. There is tension for everyone involved, the new parents, the child or children and the case worker for the adoption.

The most exciting case I ever had was a family who came down and we had just the child they had put in for. They wanted this child because they had been disappointed with another placement. It was winter time and everybody was so excited this lady forgot her coat. And it was cold weather. I sent it to her later. It worked out real well. I felt very good over that adoption.

I had one that failed. I believe we were rushed into it. There was a lady who was traveling through here. She came to our agency with her three daughters. We had never met her before that day. She decided she was going to give her kids up for adoption. She told me she had planned what she was going to do before she left home. She had separated her clothes from the children's, had her husband's death certificate, and the birth certificates of the children. She insisted she was going to leave the children that day. She was in her thirties and her daughters were twelve, eight and six years old. I talked with her for one hour. I called my supervisor down and we also discussed her request for some time. We talked to the director. He begged her to let us put the kids in foster care for a while until she could really make up her mind. She hadn't even told the children! That was a heartbreaking task to tell the children they were going to be placed in a home and were to be adopted. She gave them up so we placed them together in a home.

My rule was not to separate brothers and sisters—to keep them together whenever possible. When they are separated from their biological parents, if I could find a family that would take all the children, I wouldn't split them up. I never split up one family during my tenure with the agency. These children were Anglo and we placed them for adoption in what we perceived to be a good Anglo home. The family accepted them and it appeared to be a good placement. However, they had no experience with teen-age children. They were a church-going family and they took the children with them to services. They really wanted the children and had put in for adoption. They had two younger children of their own but they wanted more. Now there were two eight-year olds in the family and that's a no-no in my book. This family kept the three girls for a while and tried hard for a harmonious relationship, but it just didn't work. We had to place the children somewhere else. The adjustment to the extended family was more than the new mother of the three girls could take. Later we placed the three of them together in a foster home in another county.

About a year went by and we got a call from the children's mother's social worker in another state. She said the mother wanted her children back. Just luckily, the children hadn't been finally adopted so the mother got her daughters returned to her. I saw two of them a year later. They came to visit the former foster home here. We met at the coffee shop and it was nice to talk to the children. We found out the mother was an alcoholic. We just couldn't know what her problem was the first time we talked with her. She did get help at a clinic and it all ended happily after about two years.

It took a considerable amount of persuasion, but Mary Masters finally agreed to give us her recipe for dinner rolls. The recipe doesn't include the tender loving care and special touch that Mary puts into the rolls she bakes.

~~~~~~

Mary Hendricks Masters and her husband, Alfred, are now retired and live in Las Cruces. Mary is a full-time volunteer involved with the American Association of Retired Persons, the Women's Improvement Association, the Sun Country Striders, and church work, to list a few. Several mornings each week you will find her doing one of her favorite things--quilting at the Munson Center. In spite of her busy life, she always finds time to help friends and neighbors.
~~~~~~

*Mary Masters —
doing what she loves —quilting.*

Mary's Sweet Rolls

2 packages yeast,
    compressed or dry
1/2 cup lukewarm water
1/4 cup butter or margarine
3/4 cup scalded milk
1/2 cup sugar
1 teaspoon salt
2 eggs, beaten
5 cups sifed flour (about)

Soften yeast in lukewarm water. Scald milk, add butter, sugar
and salt and cool to lukewarm. Add flour to make a thick bat-
ter, then add yeast and eggs and beat well. Add enough flour to
make a soft dough that can be kneaded. Turn out onto a lightly
floured board and knead until smooth and satiny. Place in a
lightly greased bowl, cover and let rise until double in bulk,
about two hours. When light, punch down and shape as desired.
Let rise until double, 1/2 to 3/4 hour, and bake in a 350-degree
F. oven for 25 to 30 minutes for coffee cakes, 20 to 25 minutes
for rolls. This will make 2 coffee cakes or 3 dozen rolls.

Tatsue Murakami Matsusaki Tashiro

OMOIDE NO HATAKE -

GARDEN OF MEMORIES

Rose Tashiro Mitamura

Rose Tashiro Mitamura told me stories about her mother, Tatsue Murakami Matsusaki Tashiro, her three sisters, her step-father, half-brother and step-brother, as well as other family members, in May 1991. They are a rich blend of Japanese customs and the fulfillment of the American dream. The narratives demonstrate the strength, capability, and determination of the men and women in her family.

My mother was born in the southern islands of Japan in an area called Kumamoto. She came to the United States as a picture bride. She was twenty-two years old. My father, Takizo Matsusaki—they called him Tom—was born in Japan and farmed in Colorado. They had exchanged pictures and corresponded. In 1913, he sent for her and she came by ship from Japan to San Francisco and then to Colorado where they were married.

In Japan my mother worked in a place where they took the silk from the cocoon for silk thread. She brought a cocoon with her when she came from Japan and again brought one when she came to New Mexico. She showed us how she did this intricate task. Her hands were very small and soft. She was only four feet eight and one-half inches tall.

My father, a sickly man, was in and out of the hospital a lot. To support her family, my mother, the little Japanese lady with the soft hands, had to learn how to farm, raise vegetables and work in the fields. They had horses and she cultivated, plowed, harrowed and planted vegetables, sugar beets and some grain.

After harvesting them she would load her wagon, hitch up her horses and take a load of whatever was in season to the market in Denver. Many times she almost lost the wagon load because the trains would go by and frighten the horses.

Mother knew no English so she would use signs to communicate. She bartered with neighbors, trading her produce for eggs and chickens.

Mother struggled for sixteen years on that farm. My father had asthma so bad. He was in and out of the hospital so many times mother would have to borrow money to pay the bills. He had bad tonsils too but they couldn't operate on his tonsils because of his asthma. In those days they didn't have the knowledge and skills in medicine they have now. He passed away in 1928 when he was about fifty. I never knew my father because I was only nine months old when he died. I had four sisters. Toshiko was the oldest, then there was Kumi, Tsuyuko —everybody called her Sue, and Mieko. Mother had the five of us to raise and provide for. She was always busy. My older sisters took care of the younger ones so mother could do the farming and take care of the business.

After my father's death, Mother was ready to go back to Japan. She hadn't written to her mother in Japan for seven years and Grandmother thought her daughter had died. Mother wrote to her then, telling Grandmother we were coming. She had us all ready to go, even had our passports.

Kuniji Tashiro, he was always called Kay, was a close friend of my father. He too was farming in Colorado. Father had told Kay that he wanted him to take care of his family if anything ever happened to him. Kay said to my mother, "Tatsue, don't go back to Japan." He persuaded her to stay in Colorado so we did. A short time later mother and Kay Tashiro were married.

Kay had been married before when he was in Japan but his wife had died. He had a son, Harry. My sisters and I have always called Kay Tashiro father, and thought of Harry as our brother. Kay was very good to us. When he and mother were first married he was farming, raising cantaloupe in Colorado. In 1927, he took a job with the Standard Fruit Company in the Mesilla Valley. He was to develop and oversee the raising of cantaloupe. That year our family moved to the Southwest. Kay worked for the fruit company until it folded. The company failed because there was so much blight on the cantaloupe that every year they lost the crop.

Mother told me that living on a manager's salary wasn't enough and she thought she could have done better in Colorado. She said "I'm going to start farming here in New Mexico." That's what she did. Eventually, my step-father quit working for the fruit company and they farmed together. They started in the San Miguel-Mesquite area and then moved to Mesilla in 1936. They raised onions, lettuce and other vegetables. It was later they included cantaloupe on a large scale.

Times were very hard. Our lives were changing so fast. My oldest sister, Toshiko married Harry, my step-father's son. That was very hard for me to understand when I was young. They lived in Colorado when they were first married. Then they moved to the Mesilla Valley and started farming here.

Kumi (l.) and Mieko Tashiro ready to take a load of produce to El Paso.

My older sisters were in school then and they used to have to get up very early, load the vegetables and take them to market in El Paso and get back on time for school. They attended Las Cruces High School and one year at Valley High, which is now Gadsden. The girls worked the fields with the horses, cultivating and then harvesting and processing the crops.

Mitamura

The first house we lived in when we moved here was an adobe house with those roofs of mud and cattails. Things kept dropping out of the ceiling so my dad decided it was time to build a house for us. He built a two-bedroom rock house. Imagine a house that small for all of us! There was a porch on it which he filled in and that's where we slept. It got awfully cold out there in the winter time and we would put hot water bottles in the bed to keep us warm. The funniest thing was that after he had the house built there was only one door to go in and out of. They had to tear down a place in the wall for another door.

Rose Mitamura's mother did not forget the ancient customs of the Japanese and felt it her duty to tell her children about them. Adapting to an alien way of life in the desert Southwest must have been more difficult for Tatsue Tashiro than anyone realized.

Mother told us the Japanese have ancient customs about the sons in the family. My mother had a brother and a sister. The brother had no children so he took one of the sister's daughters under his name as his daughter. When she married, her husband would take her father's family name to carry on the name. That was the tradition in Japan at that time. I don't know if they follow that tradition now but when my brother George was born we learned about it first hand.

My step-father, Kay, was sixty years old, when my mother gave birth to a son. People would not believe that, at last, after five daughters, mother had a son! She would prove to her friends that she had a boy. They called him George, and wow! Did my mother spoil him. He was her eyes she used to tell us.[1] "If you hurt him you hurt me." She doted on him. I was two when he was born but when we girls were growing up, I think I sensed some jealousy. I understood, but some of my sisters still have resentment.

In 1937, when George was six years old, mother and dad took him to Japan to show him off. They stayed a month and when they came back he had forgotten all his English and he was bowing to us and all that. We thought that was strange. She took him to Japan again when he was grown to find a wife

---

[1] The Japanese equivalent of the English, "You are my pride and joy."

but he wasn't interested. At that time mother demanded that we marry our own. She thought some of the young Japanese women in Colorado or Texas would be all right for George but he didn't agree with her. We girls all married Japanese but George didn't.

Mother always worried about George. After he graduated from New Mexico State University, then New Mexico College of Agriculture & Mechanic Arts, in 1951, with a degree in Agriculture and an Air Force Commission as Second Lieutenant, he was sent to Walker Air Force Base in Roswell, New Mexico. George had hoped and dreamed of being sent far, far away but, no, he wound up in Roswell. He really enjoyed his two years in the Air Force. The fact that he was a lieutenant in the Air Force didn't stop mother from worrying. When he left for Roswell mother didn't hear from him for two weeks, so she had Sue call to find out if he was all right.

You see, the Japanese custom is that the son gets everything. They gave George so much and we girls had to work along with our parents—accumulating what they had with sweat and blood. I grew up accepting it and still help my brother as much as I can. I have helped him with his children because he has had problems with his family, a bad marriage and divorce.   My husband and I raised George's two younger children after he was divorced. We adopted them and they lived with us until they were grown. The girl, who is twenty-three now, sent me a card on Mother's Day and wrote on it that she appreciated what I had done for her. That made me feel good. Through all the years we have done what we could for him. Eventually, with all his problems, he lost all the land my parents had given him. That just broke my mother's heart. That was the biggest disappointment in her life.

It is understandable that Rose Mitamura's mother would want to follow the traditions of her Japanese ancestors when Rose related about her grandmother's heritage.

My mother used to tell us that my grandmother was of royal blood. Blue blood is what she used to say. One time one of my nephews saw her cut her hand and he said, "Oh, I thought Grandma's blood was blue. It's red, just like our's." We never did find out exactly the origin of the royal blood line but my mother's father was a wealthy landowner at one time. Mother said her father used to drink a lot. In Japan in those days they used a seal for your signature. People would get our grandfather drunk and he would sign over his land. Finally, he lost all the land that he owned. Mother said then they were impoverished, so she had to go to work. The oldest in her family was a daughter, Mother was the middle one and a son came after her. The oldest one got all the nice kimonos and Mother got all the hand-me-downs. Of course the son would be favored because he was a son. Mother was really put out. She said, "I'm going to America and I'm going to make it rich and buy my own kimonos." She was determined and how she struggled for years and years to acquire what she wanted.

Tatsue Tashiro never wavered in her quest for the good life and toiled long hours to achieve her goals.

Mother was very strict and a good business woman. She used to figure with an abacus. She never let anybody make a fool of her. I wish she had taught us how to use an abacus but she was always so busy. She was very much the matriarch who told everyone what to do. When she supervised the workers from Mexico she would call out, "Andale, andale!" [hurry, hurry] if they were not working fast enough. They would have a hard time keeping up with mother who worked beside them hoeing or picking. Her Japanese-Mexican-English language was really something, but she made herself understood. She might stop and roll herself a cigarette with her Bull Durham tobacco, but she expected the men to keep on working. She really cracked the whip when she worked the men. She didn't want them to stop. She couldn't remember their names so she would say, the tall skinny one, or the dark one. We would have to figure out who she was talking about. Kay, my father was the salesman of the family operation. While mother and Harry were in the fields, he was making trips to El Paso selling what we raised.

My mother and father were consistently trying to better themselves. Kay was unable to get a formal education in Japan when he was young because he had to take care of his younger brothers. When he came here he would study one Japanese character every night. He said, "If I learn one character each day, I will learn three hundred and sixty-five characters in a year." That's what he did. He would write to his relatives in Japan. He learned a lot by teaching himself.

There were many things to overcome. I remember the years we had the big rains and we had to ride the horse to get around the farm. It was my job to milk the goat and cow and help in the fields. My older sisters worked especially hard while they were in school. Mother worked with horses until the Forties. There were many lean years but mother, my step-father, my step-brother Harry, and my sisters, we all worked together to make what we hoped for a reality.

My sister Kumi, wanted to go to college. It was really tough to come up with the $100 for tuition, but my folks managed somehow and she went to the University of Colorado at Boulder. She lived in a basement and worked in the university restaurant in the kitchen to make extra money. She got a degree in pharmacy in 1940. Kumi stayed in Colorado, working for a while in Denver and Colorado Springs. Then World War II broke out. Kumi knew that her step-father was very loyal to his adopted country, but he was sad because he had no sons to give to serve in the United States Army. So my sister volunteered for the WAC [Women's Army Corps]. They had to waiver her in because, like my mother, she was very short—not five feet tall. She was thin and ate bananas to gain weight. When she was sworn into the WACs it made my father very happy because he wanted someone from the family to be represented in the service. After the war was over Kumi married and moved to Los Angeles with her husband.

In 1941, when the war broke out, I started school at Court Junior High School. That was when they first opened it up. The building wasn't even finished. Just because we looked Japanese people didn't seem to realize that we were born in America and were Americans. I have never been to Japan. There were other students of Japanese background like myself in school. Once in a while other students would call us "Japs," which irritated us.

In addition to all the hardships connected with the farming at that time, discrimination reared its ugly head in a big way in the valley. Rose narrated how her family reacted to the touchy situation.

The Japanese were denied citizenship until 1953 when our parents became naturalized citizens. In the early 1940's after World War II started, a group of people here tried to form a county-wide organization to "keep alien Japs from colonizing in Doña Ana County." The poster they ran in the newspaper announced that a mass meeting would be held in the court house on October first and asked that people attend the meeting and give their moral support. This occurred when my sister, Sue Tashiro Yanaga, bought land from a local real estate dealer. The real estate dealer was accused of bringing alien Japanese into the valley. He defended his actions saying that, "the two local Japanese families have lived here for more than twenty years. Suki (Sue) Tashiro Yanaga's husband is a World War II veteran, wounded and discharged after fighting on the Italian front. He was born in Colorado. These two families have bought and owned land here for over twenty years."

An interesting incident happened the other day in the branch post office that I run. A lady came in and she told me her uncle was a newspaper reporter here in Las Cruces at that time and fairly new in the area. She said he got up at the meeting and asked those in attendance why they were meeting. He defended our family by saying that we worked hard, minded our own business, didn't bother anyone and had been living here for years. Someone else expressed the same facts and pretty soon one by one the meeting disbanded.

The whole affair was disgusting to the family and we were really appalled that they would come up with something like that after all the years we had lived here. We realized we were not as bad off during the war as the other Japanese were on the West Coast. Officers did come to our home and they took our guns and radio. They were afraid that we would aid the enemy, I guess. None of the confiscated items were ever returned to us.

During the war years there was an incident when my dad and Harry went to El Paso to a baseball game. They were picked up and arrested because they were not supposed to be outside of a radius of twenty, or maybe it was thirty, miles from their home. They were thrown in jail and my dad told us they served them oatmeal for breakfast the next morning, but didn't give them a spoon to eat it with so he used his baseball ticket for a spoon. They were released that day.

Our bank deposits were frozen. Our friends helped us out and their kindness will be remembered forever. The D. C.

Frietze family, who owned a grocery store in Mesilla, helped us through those difficult times and through the lean years by letting us have groceries on credit. Mr. Willis Buckley, who had the Thrift Grocery Store on Main Street in Las Cruces, was also very good to us. He said, "Don't worry. You can come and charge all the groceries you need until they get it all straightened out." After all the restrictions were lifted we could carry on our business, which we did. My mother's principles, which she taught us, were to work hard and mind our own business.

Rose reminisced about her youth and the direction her life took after she graduated from high school.

I told my mother, "I'm going to college." She said, "There's no use sending girls to college because they get married and then you have wasted all that money." But I was insistent. I told mother I wanted to major in business administration so I could be her shipper. She finally relented and I went. After three semesters I quit. I was in love with Bob Mitamura. He lived in Colorado and was a friend of my sister Sue's husband. He had come out to work for my dad two winters and then entered the service. He didn't ship out with his outfit because his papers were lost for a time. He was lucky in one way because many of his outfit were killed in battle. He guarded German prisoners while he was in the service. He came back to Colorado after he was discharged and took up the farming he had left when he entered the service. We had corresponded for four years before we married.

I was supposedly going to school one morning but Bob and I eloped to El Paso and were married by a judge. We had to pull him out of the courtroom. We didn't tell anybody but it came out in the paper and one of the workers in the produce house said to my dad, "I see your daughter got married." My dad came home and told my mother and boy, oh boy, did I get it! After it all cooled down, my mother demanded that Bob go back to Colorado and bring somebody to represent his family —Japanese style. Mother wanted what the Japanese call, "a go-between." In the old days, even in this country, the Japanese would have their good friend talk to this parent to see if their daughter or son would want to marry the other parent's son or daughter. That was the way many of marriages were arranged in the old, old days. The Japanese custom was brought to this country by the older folks. This was already after our marriage, but mother still demanded that.

Bob went back to Colorado and brought his father and the family friend. They talked about our marriage and it was okayed. My father was the diplomat in the family. He arranged the reception for us. Mother was as usual, busy with the farm. At that time there was no really nice place that was big enough for a reception so it was held in the Tortugas Cafe at the bus stop on Main Street in Las Cruces. We had a cake and they toasted the bride and groom, American style. When we went back to Colorado his family had a reception for us. They had a large community of Japanese there and they gathered together, brought food, drank a lot of Sake, sang and had a good time.

We lived in Colorado for two years. My husband was farming with his family but it was not easy or very profitable there. In Colorado the hail would come and wipe out the crops completely. The market wasn't that good either. My mother came to visit us several times. Every time she came she said I looked skinnier and she was worried about me. She thought I was too thin. She came home and told my dad. My dad was very good to me. He said, "We better bring them back here to farm." Bob didn't want to come to New Mexico because he was the oldest son and had to take care of his parents. I told him we can help them more if we are successful farming in New Mexico. So we moved here and we did help them out. My folks set us up with a loan and credit where we needed it and got us started. We worked hard. It took us a few years, but we paid them back.

I had two miscarriages before my oldest daughter Sharon was born in 1953, and I almost lost her. My second daughter, Karen was premature and weighed a little more than four pounds when she was born. She was in an incubator and when we brought her home I had to put on a mask to feed her and be so careful for over a year. We did get her raised and she is fine. My son, Richard was born two years later, a healthy strong baby. I continued helping out in the fields when the children were growing up just as my mother did.

The family continued farming in the Mesilla Valley. The business operation known as Tashiro Farms became very successful but only after a lot of blood, sweat, and tears.

As the years went by, Mama Tashiro and her husband could enjoy some of the benefits of their years of hard work, but being idle was not part of their lifestyle.

Both my mother and father made several trips to Japan while he was still alive. However, in 1956 Kay was in an automobile accident. He was by himself on the way to one of the farms. He fractured his ribs and wound up with pneumonia. He got out of the hospital but never seemed to fully recover. I think he sensed that death was coming. One day he went to say good-by to some of the people he knew when he first came to the valley. I understand that he rolled the truck into a ditch or something and he hit his ribs again where he had fractured them before and he just didn't make it. He lived to be eighty-three. He had come to the United States when he was very young but mother remembered he said a palmist in Japan had told him he would live to be eighty-three and I think he may have thought, "this is it." The family doctor said, "He just seemed to give up."

We had another death in the family—my oldest sister, Toshiko, who had married Harry, died in 1941. She left three daughters. We all helped Harry raise the girls.

Mother went back to Japan to see her family several times after Dad died. She helped them in many ways. She added on rooms to my grandmother's house and gave her things that would make living more comfortable for her. She helped her sister who had lost a son. My aunt snapped out of her depression when my mother came to visit. My grandmother lived to be ninety-two or three. Then Mother's sister died and her only brother was killed. Mother brought some of her relatives to visit us here but they all went back to Japan. Mother was a helper and if she were alive today, I'm sure she would be helping someone somewhere.

Rose laughed when she spoke of what her mother did after she retired.

My mother fought retirement all the way. She continued raising vegetables for about four or five years in a little plot in front of her house. That's the house that my dad wanted to retire in. He called it his dream house. The night before he

Tatsue Tashiro's mother on her porch in Japan.

passed away we understand he went to the carpenter and asked him to fix up his room so he could spend one night in it. He seemed to have a premonition that he was going to leave this world. That was in August 1956 and the house wasn't finished until the last of the year. I bought the house when the estate was settled because I wanted it to stay in the family. The house is our home now and there are usually grandchildren and other family members coming to stay for a while.

What Rose said about her mother's activities and attitude reenforces the legend that Mama Tashiro was a diligent, resourceful woman who overcame difficulties and challenges all her life.

My mother was always close to us girls. As is the Japanese custom, the son is supposed to take care of his parents. As Mother grew older she realized that her son, George, wouldn't be able to do that. She became even closer to all of us and felt that even though we were women, we were very important. She kind of doted on my son, but she loved all my kids. She never did baby-sit though. She was busy, busy, busy. She became a fishing enthusiast. Every chance she had she would go to Elephant Butte and fish.

Another bit of my mother's philosophy was she believed that idleness is bad for the mind. When she retired after more than fifty years of active farming she learned how to make Japanese ceremonial dolls. "If there is no work, you just sleep, and your head gets empty," she would say. Her material for the dolls included silk brocade, doll torsos, head and limbs, fans, hair, swords and musical instruments as well as head ornaments and hats. She brought them back with her from Japan.

When Rose talked about herself retiring it was like an echo of her mother's voice.

When Bob and I retired from farming about five years ago I said, "I'm not going to stay home." I went to work as a cook at Tatsu, a Japanese restaurant and worked there full-time for over five years and, at the same time, worked in the kitchen at the Ming Palace part-time. When the opportunity came up to run the branch post office in the Ming Palace I said, "I'll take a crack at it." I bid on it and got it. I like doing what I do there and it surprises me because I was shy. I didn't know what to say to people. I would want to hide when people came to visit. You wouldn't believe it now! This has been good for me and I enjoy it. I got over my shyness. I still help out on weekends in the kitchen at the Ming Palace. I like to be busy.

Our conversation turned to music and another of Mama Tashiro's talents came into focus.

My mother used to play an instrument called the samisen. It's like a banjo with a long neck and three strings. When her folks were affluent in Japan she took lessons on the samisen and Japanese dancing lessons—called Odori. She never taught us but when she lived in Colorado the Japanese groups would always have some sort of festival. They begged her to come and teach the dance. Mother said she was carrying me and told them, "How can I teach dancing when I look like this?" They assured her that was okay, to come anyway. So she went. The Japanese have a way of not paying directly but showing their appreciation by way of a gift. They did give her money for a gift and she said she really appreciated it. That was when my father was sick and she had so many mouths to feed. That's why she was so happy when my daughter began to play violin and piano and my second daughter and son played instruments. She thought if all else failed, they could use their musical talent to make a living. I still have the samisen but it needs repair. Mother never played much here because the Japanese have no social center and of course, she was more involved with her business.

During her retirement years Tatsue Tashiro became known as "Grandma Tashiro." The energetic, good-hearted, and capable business woman who spent fifty-five years farming well deserved her incomparable reputation.

When Mother had her eighty-eighth birthday, her six children, including myself, gave her a big celebration. Relatives came from Colorado, California, all over. Some of our relatives came from Japan. In Japan, a person's eighty-eighth birthday has special significance. It is a custom dating back to the ages when it was very rare for a person to live to be that old. It was believed that at eighty-eight a person is reborn again and the celebration hinges on the long life of the turtle and the crane. All the families together made a thousand and one cranes. The cranes are made out of paper. The art work is called "Origami" —which means folded paper. On her birthday the cranes were all strung together and it was a beautiful thing. The saying in Japan is, "A turtle can live a hundred years but the crane lives a thousand." It symbolizes long life. Mother had a long and eventful life, but she died in 1979 a few months after her 88th birthday. At that time she had twenty-two grandchildren and two great-grandchildren. Her Buddhist name, Shaku Ni Jisho, is shown on her "In Memory of" card as well as her given name, Tatsue Tashiro.

Rose related how her father and mother were Buddhists and explained the ceremonies that the Buddhists conduct after death.

We followed the custom of the Buddhist religion after our mother's and father's deaths. A family representative goes to a Buddhist temple on the forty-ninth day after the death for a memorial service. This memorial service is repeated again on the first year, the third year and it goes on to the thirteenth

*Tatsue "Mama" Tashio with her family on her 88th birthday.
Clockwise: Mieko, George, Rose, Sue and Kumi.*

year. We all went to Denver for the third year ceremony. The Buddhist consider that on the day of your death you have been dead one year, so they calculate the first year as the second anniversary of death. Our temple, the Tri-State Buddhist Church, is in Denver. Now my brother can't go so we send money to the church and they have the service said for our family members.

In the Tashiro home we had a room where the family worshiped. My dad had an inscribed piece of bark written by a person like a saint. It was given to my father in Japan. He was very honored and proud to have received it. He was to pass it down to the next oldest in his family, which is Harry. When Harry passes away he will pass it on to his oldest—a daughter.

When my dad was alive we practiced the Buddhist religion. On New Year's Day we would have to get up early in the morning. He would light the candles in the room and we would bow and say a Buddhist prayer. When Buddhists visit the cemetery they burn incense at the grave. I put on flowers. The Buddhist priest comes from Denver once a year and gives a service by the tombstones at the grave site of our relatives. After the service, Harry, the oldest son takes the priest and the family out to dinner. Buddhism isn't practiced so much here like it is in Denver where there is a large community of Japanese.

~~~~~~~

Tatsue Tashiro and her five daughters are truly valiant survivors of the difficult years when the Southwest was young.

~~~~~~~

Tashiko Matsusaki Tashiro, (Harry Tashiro's wife) died in 1941.

Kumi Matsusaki Ishizawa died in California in 1984. (Her husband, Harold Ishizawa lived in Los Angeles, was evacuated to a re-location camp and eventually moved to Denver during World War II.)

The three youngest daughters were adopted by their step-father, Kay Tashiro.

Tsuyuko Tashiro Yanaga lives in Las Cruces, New Mexico.

Mieko Tashiro Mayeda lives in Brighton, Colorado. (Her husband, Roy Mayeda, was a Captain in the US Army)

Rose Tashiro Mitamura and her husband Bob, live in Mesilla, New Mexico.

George Tashiro lives in Las Vegas, Nevada.

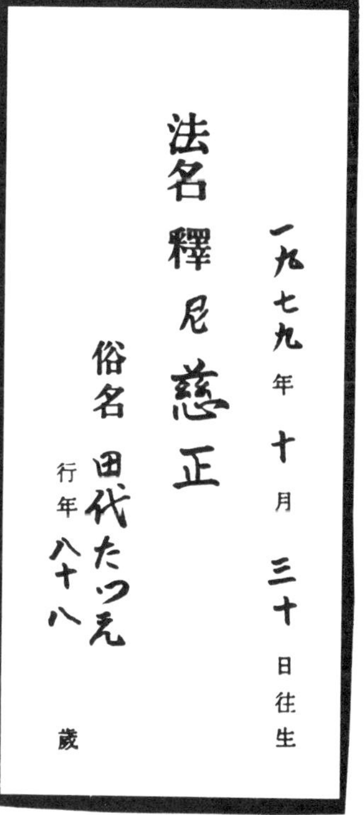

Tatsue Tashiro's In Memory Card

Hester Day Roach

$\mathcal{V}$ANGUARD IN THE VALLEY

Hester Day Roach

*In 1983, when Hester Day Roach began reflecting on her yes-
terdays, it was apparent that her parents' experiences when they
came to New Mexico from the East influenced her throughout her
lifetime. As a first-generation Southwestern woman she pridefully
told stories about years gone by—always tempering them with
humor and compassion.*

My father was Elias Day. He graduated from Tufts College
near Boston. He and two of his friends, Jack Tarr and a fellow
by the name of Penrose (who built the Broadmor Hotel in
Colorado) went to Washington. D.C. While they were there
they read in the Congressional Library how they could make a
million dollars raising onions in the Mesilla Valley of New
Mexico Territory. The three decided they would come to Las
Cruces. It was in 1887 or 1888—I'm not sure of the year.
My father's father was a sea captain. He owned his own
ship and used to go to China and different places but he didn't
have a lot of money. He'd have money for a while after he
returned from a voyage. But he wasn't a rich man by any
means. Anyway, my father, wanted to make it on his own. So
he and the two other boys came here and bought a farm and
raised onions. They had the Mexicans doing all the work, etc.
They bought horses and beautiful saddles and many other
things. That lasted about three years and then they were broke.
They sold the land and divided the profits. Jack Tarr went back
to Boston and when I was in the third or fourth grade I studied
a geography that he had written. Penrose, the other man, went
to Colorado. He made many fortunes in mining—millions of
dollars. His son married a good friend of my sister Grace, who

lived in Colorado at that time. Grace kept up with that part of the story for years. But my father stayed here. He often told us he never had money enough to get out of town.

Before they were married, when my father was here in New Mexico and my mother was in Boston, father wrote long letters to her telling about New Mexico and the people who lived here. His letters were beautifully poetic and mother must have cherished them because she brought them with her when she came here as a bride.

This is the last paragraph of a letter dated May 28, 1893, to Grace Center from Elias Day:

> My dear Grace,
>
> ...How much I would have enjoyed that walk with you in the moonlight! The moon here is beautiful tonight and one can read a newspaper out of doors it is so clear and bright. Such a moon and such pleasant nights always make me think of old times, old Gloucester, and old friends. There is a tinge of sentiment in me and there is nothing like moonlight to bring it out. I sit for a long time and gaze upon that moon and dream. Scores of happy evenings long since gone came before my mind, and thoughts of nobler, purer, gentler things come over me. The devils in the moon for mischief may be true, but certainly there is that in its soft calm light which calls up the good in man and leads his thoughts in nobler channels, to think of God, of love, of heaven and home. And thus it is with me. And in this mood I will leave you. Good night, my Grace, and with my whole heart and soul believe me.
>
> Yours,
>
> Elias

Later, in 1893, my father went back East and he and my mother were married. Then he brought her to New Mexico. They stopped in El Paso. The trains were running here then. My father, Elias, had a college nickname of "Nubby", and everyone back East used to call him that. He was quite a baseball player. Mother said, "Elias, I don't think I can stand it, if Las Cruces is anything like El Paso." He said, "Oh, it isn't anything like El Paso." 'Course El Paso was pretty civilized then. She said, "There is just one consolation in going to Las

Cruces, they won't call you Nubby Day. I just can't stand that."

They got here at the station and of course, everybody knew he was coming with his new bride. The whole town was down there to meet 'em. The first thing she heard was, "Hello, Mrs. Nubby!"

I don't think mother had ever been west of Chicago and you can imagine her thoughts. This was the wild and woolly west to her.

Her father was collector of customs at the Port of Gloucester at the time. That port is northeast of Boston. When she was going to get married, she went down to Boston for a month to learn how to cook. She was a wonderful cook. Mama got so she loved it here but she never lost her New England accent. She was really a marvelous character. To just pick up and move out here in those days took a lot of courage.

There was a lumber yard in Las Cruces, across from the old post office. The F. H. Bascomb Company used to construct all the buildings here. When you see an older red brick house you know that the Bascomb Company built it. My father got in with Mr. Bascomb. He taught the two Ruiz brothers how to do the carpentry and plumbing and those two worked for the Bascomb Company for as long as they lived.

It took considerable strength and self-discipline for Elias Day's wife and daughters to maintain the lifestyle he had provided for them before his death.

I had two sisters. Ruth was the older and Grace was younger than I was. My father died in 1908 and we were always in a depression. We never had enough money. When father died he owned stock in the F.H. Bascomb Company. The whole time we were going to school, mother would be taking money out of the company—selling a little more stock each time. Before I got out of school that was used up. That's why I always gave mother half of what I earned. She owned the house we lived in on Griggs Street. That's where I was born and I think it is still there.

I went to college in 1916 up to the spring of 1917 when they closed the college in March because all the boys left to fight Pancho Villa, who was coming up from Mexico. I never went back to college. I went to work for the Bowman Bank and Trust. I did everything—bookkeeping, cashier, wrote letters.

Blanche Frenger Cox, who was a friend of mine, worked there too. Her father was president of the bank and I think that's why we got jobs. We got over $100 a month and that was an excellent salary for then. I was giving my mother some of my salary, like I said, because I lived at home and being a widow she needed the money. I worked there until I was married.

I knew Paul Roach before he was drafted into the US Army in the First World War. He was a customer at the Bowman Bank were I worked. I had another boyfriend who also went to war, but I married Paul. He was in Europe and seriously wounded in the face just two days before the Armistice was signed. He spent time in one of those plush hotels in France trying to get his face back together again. He didn't come home until 1919.

In 1920 we were married in the Community House here. It was a two-story house where the [St. Paul's United] Methodist Church is now. Some friends of ours were running it – the George Frengers. I wore a long dress. There was no train on it. It was the same dress that Blanche Cox wore when she was married to Raymond Frenger. We had an orchestra there and when we left they all danced. It was a big dance and we went on down to El Paso.

When we were first married my husband worked for the West Texas Fuel Company. He used to buy alfalfa for them. We lived in El Paso for about three months and then moved up on Paul's farm. It was a hundred and twenty acres at Hill, New Mexico. He farmed it and he also raised chickens and we sold eggs. The third day we were up there we got one hundred and twenty-five baby chicks. We had no place to put them or anything else. So in the morning we spread them out on the front porch on papers. When night time came we had to take all those little chicks and put them back in the box. We finally got a place all fixed up. Of course, he raised chickens for the eggs. He did that before we were married so he knew all about it, but it was new to me.

We built up our chicken population until it was about eighteen hundred hens. I remember the first eggs we shipped out to a Mr. Yearwood down in El Paso. He had two or three grocery stores. The first full box we sent down, was twelve dozen eggs. This was the winter of 1920. I can't remember exactly how much we got for them, but with what it cost us to feed the chickens, we couldn't even commence to make any profit. We lived on the farm until about 1923.

We never had any money. Fortunately, our expenses were not very high. Our first baby, Kilborn, came in the fall of 1921. I remember our doctor bill was about $25. He was born at my sister's home. Dr. McBride delivered him. Dr. McBride, sweet, old Dr. McBride that everybody knew and loved. He delivered my other baby, Paul Jr., too.

In 1923, Paul got a job as ditchrider in this area. We moved to Doña Ana and leased out the farm. In 1920 cotton was just beginning to be raised here in the valley. My husband had three acres of cotton. He harvested three bales and got sixteen cents a pound for it. That would hardly pay for picking the cotton! We had no trouble getting cotton pickers because men had a hard time getting a job any place else. I don't remember what we paid to have them pick the cotton but I do know we didn't make any money raising cotton.

Paul worked himself up to be watermaster with the Bureau of Reclamation. He had charge of irrigation in the whole valley from El Paso to Elephant Butte until about 1927.

Our second son was born in 1927 and it was a year of changes for us. A man from northern New Mexico, came into Paul's office and said, "I'm looking for a man that knows all about irrigation. We are about to build a dam in northwestern New Mexico and I want a man to look at it." My husband said, "You're lookin' at the best one in the world." So the man offered Paul the job. Paul said, "I'd have to talk to my wife to see if she would go up there first." Paul had me to take care of and a baby two days old. The man said he wouldn't look any further and Paul could come up and look at it.

Paul waited until the next day before he told me about it. Mr. James Edgar Haines, the grandfather of the family that still lives in Las Cruces, was an old friend of our family. He used to live in the part of New Mexico where they were going to build the dam. My husband talked him into taking him up there to look over that irrigation district. It's funny how things happen. On the way back Mr. Haines said, "You don't want to go up there. Why don't you buy my store at Doña Ana." Paul said, "I don't have any money. I'd have to pay you little by little." Mr. Haines said, "That's perfectly all right." And that's how we bought the Doña Ana Mercantile Store. There were no papers signed just an agreement between two men.

Paul wrote the man that he wouldn't take the job because he was going to run the store at Doña Ana. My husband still had a job with the West Texas Fuel Company. It was just a little buying trip every now and then.

Our store was the only one in Doña Ana. Most of our customers were Mexicans and they traded there whether they had any money or not. If they needed shoes and he didn't have them Paul would get their size and purchase them in Las Cruces for them. Nobody ever beat him out of money. Paul seemed to have an affinity for the Mexicans. He could speak Spanish and was their "daddy." If they ever had any trouble they would come to Paul. Some had little farms, but their farms were too small to raise cotton so they worked for the farmers who did raise cotton.

I remember during the Depression years when we had the store everybody charged things. I said to my husband, "You're getting in awfully deep." He said, "I'm not worried about getting paid. If the Mexicans have any money, they will pay me back."

I think it was in the late Twenties, Paul decided he wanted to get out of the store. A man bought him out and I don't know whether that man ever got the money owned or not.

For years after we left Doña Ana, Paul never forgot the Mexican families in Doña Ana. On Christmas Eve he would go to the manager of the J C Penney Store here and persuade him to give all the toys he hadn't sold to the poor. Paul would take the toys out to the shacks where the Mexicans lived in Doña Ana and give the toys to the children. He would take whiskey for the men. My husband would say, "No, I no Santa Claus, I, Paul Roach." He would do the same thing in Old Mesilla. All the men wanted Paul to have a drink of the whiskey with them so by the time he got home on Christmas Eve he was feeling mighty full of Christmas spirit. He saw the farm laborers through the Depression and other hard years.

When Paul was in politics he gave many a speech on the Plaza in Old Mesilla. His Mexican friends remembered him when he was running for office.

Hester Roach spoke knowingly about churches and how they were built even when the area was sparsely populated. She remembered how the social life of the community was centered around the church. Most women in the area at that time were not interested in politics or economic conditions.

All the people around Hill got together many years ago and built the little fieldstone church that is still standing. Actually, a Dr. Charles Lee Hill was the first one who thought about it. He was a retired dentist who moved out here from back East somewhere. The Walters and the Haines and quite a few other families around there put in money and hired someone to build it. It cost $5,000. It was around 1923 or '24.

I belonged to the Presbyterian Church in Las Cruces and some of us younger women wanted a group of our own. A lot of them were school teachers and we decided we would meet at four o'clock in the afternoon and have refreshments and get someone to speak. That group is still going strong except we have changed the time.

Every Thanksgiving and Christmas we would have special meetings and tell each member to bring at least two things, two cans of something or a package of beans and then we would make up baskets and take them out to poor. We did that for many years.

Dr. Hill, the little place was named for him, ran for governor back in 1920 when women first got the vote and I voted then. My husband was in politics and I always voted. One time when he was running for assessor I voted a straight Democratic ticket. I've always been a Democrat, but I vote for the best person. I used to help at the voting polls.

Those Depression years long ago were terrible. Money was awfully hard to get. We learned how to get by and that's what we did. It was surprising how women rarely talked about politics back in the Twenties. I didn't belong to many organizations except the Presbyterian Church and the PEO. When women got together they seemed to discuss families, church, sometimes music or art, and do a little gossiping.

I did work outside my home in the late Twenties. My husband was assessor then and I worked with him in the office. There was no regulation about husbands and wives working in the same office in those days. I wasn't paid much, less than $100 a month.

With an energetic husband who seemed to thrive on change, Hester was always there supporting him. If there were times when she wished things were different, she didn't complain. She was always by his side.

My husband took another job again after he had been assessor. He was appointed Register of the United States Land Office in Las Cruces. His office was in the old post office building and it was a very busy office because, for the second time, they started drilling for oil in Doña Ana County. The drilling was at the Corralitos Ranch owned by a Mr. Armstrong. That well was a dud, just like the first time they drilled for oil on the Cox Ranch in 1920. Both times all they struck was water. I had stock in the first well and I remember the certificates were kept in the bank I worked in. The bank moved to Hatch and later was brought back here, but I never did get the certificates back. I think if my husband hadn't been connected with the assessor's office he might have been involved with the oil wells.

Mrs. Roach's memories of the hard times were like many tragic events; there was always some humor sprinkled along the way. She laughed when she told about the Las Cruces bank that went broke.

The First State Bank across the street from us went broke. The fellow who owned it had built a big house on Picacho. When the bank went broke they put him in jail.

There's a funny story about Lollie Campbell who had the Campbell Hotel on Main Street. She served meals and had rooms for rent. Three times a day someone from the sheriff's office would come and pick up meals. One day she said, "Who in the world are you taking these meals to?" They told her it was the man who had been president of the bank that failed. She really bawled them out and said, "For heaven's sake, if I'd a known that, I might have put some poison in that food. Fact of the matter, I never would have made the meals in the first place!" Everybody loved Lollie and she evidently had lost some money in that bank when it went broke. She wasn't related to the Campbells that had the Amador Hotel in Las Cruces.

The closeness between Hester Roach, her mother and two sisters was expressed lovingly and undeniably. It crept into her stories naturally because they shared one another's joys and sorrows as well as pride in their accomplishments.

I said to Paul back in 1939, when he said he was going into politics, we're going to build us a house first. I talked to Mr. Hess—who owned the five lots where I wanted my house—that I wanted to buy them. He wanted $250 a lot. I said I would give him what they were assessed for, which was $100. I knew the amount from when I worked in the assessor's office. I looked it up the other day and they are assessed at $2,000 a lot now [1983]. He told me the restrictions were that we had to build a pueblo-style house. I said that was o.k. He said, "Oh, you're quite a manager. I'll sell them to you for $100 a lot."

I bought some other lots from Mr. Hess and sold one to my sister, Ruth Johns Lisle. Ruth built a house there and since Mother was alone she and Ruth lived together. It was so nice to have them close by. Ruth was always so talented. Her book, *Chickens Don't Turn To Dust,* which was published in 1968, is now included in the Rare Books Collection at New Mexico State University Library. Later years my other sister, Grace [Chance], lived in the same block so we saw each other almost every day.

I also had a house built for [William] 'Bill' O'Donnell when he moved here from Colorado to be a dean at New Mexico College of A & M.

The two Ruiz brothers built our house and the architect was Percy McGee from El Paso. He also built the old library and the county courthouse in Las Cruces. We moved in the day after Christmas in 1939. We got a bill from McGee, I forgot how much it was and he wrote across it "Merry Christmas and Happy New Year. Paid in full." So we didn't have to pay Percy anything for drawing up the plans. He would come up every week and supervise the building of the house.

Hester Roach didn't deny that having "friends in high places" and being involved in politics, was something that helped her and her husband many times when they had problems. She spoke openly about it.

My husband was a very good friend of Dennis Chavez who was United States Senator from New Mexico for many years. In fact, Senator Chavez gave my older son, Kilborn, an appointment to West Point. Paul, Jr.'s principal appointment to West Point was by Senator Hatch. He had been drafted and was at Camp Roberts, Texas when he received a second appointment from Congressman Clinton P. Anderson. He was at Amherst College for a year before entering West Point. He graduated with the Class of 1950.

When they graduate from West Point they pick out which branch of the service they want to go in and they are sent to their branch school for four or five months of training in their particular field. After his training Paul was immediately sent to Korea. Paul's class, had a high percentage of casualties.

Mrs. Roach told of the most trying times in her life with the same strength and courage she must have shown when her husband died and when her older son was wounded in one war and her younger son became a prisoner in another war.

Kilborn graduated from West Point in 1943. They rushed them through in three and one-half years because that was after World War II had started. After training in Texas he was sent to Europe. In the fall of 1944, he was wounded. It was so ironic because it was just ten miles from where my husband had been wounded in the Fall of 1918 during World War I. He came back to the states, but he was a career army man and retired as a colonel.

In 1948, my husband died. Paul Jr. was at West Point and he came home for the funeral. Kilborn got leave and came. Of course, Mama, and my sisters, Grace and Ruth, were there. We supported one another through one tragedy after another. After Paul's death, I was alone in my home but having them living nearby was comforting. We spent many hours together.

In 1952, the day after Christmas I got a telegram saying that Paul, Jr. was missing in action. I didn't hear a word from him until one morning in July, 1953. My sister Grace came driving up in her car, honking the horn. It was very early and I thought she had gone crazy. She came up the walk waving two letters in her hand. They had cone from Paul who was in a prison camp in North Korea. Of course in those days we knew everybody in the post office. One of the boys in the post office called Grace. He said, "Grace, isn't Hester's boy over in Korea?" Grace said, "He's missing somewhere but we don't know where he is." He said, "Well, there's two letters here for Mrs. Roach. And I'm afraid to call her." Grace said, "I'll be right up." She didn't even take off her nightgown. She had an upper plate she forgot to put in. She put on her bedroom slippers and her robe and she went up there and got the letters and came here. We cried and we laughed and we cried again and finally I thought I better let the rest of the family know. We went across the street and told Ruth and Mama and laughed and cried all over again. Believe me that certainly was a day I will never forget!

*Hester Roach
and son Paul, Jr.*

Paul was a prisoner over there for three years until August 1953. I went to San Francisco to meet him. They told me what ship he would be on and just exactly what to do. They wouldn't fly them home. It took twelve or fourteen days to come home and Paul gained almost thirty pounds in those days after he was released from the prison. Paul said they had steaks for breakfast and they fed them all the food that would help them gain weight and that's why they wanted to bring them back by ship. He stayed in the army and when he retired he was a colonel. He lives in Hillsboro, New Mexico now and is really having the time of his life. Kilborn is retired and lives in Maryland.

Hester Roach with one of her great-grand-children, Paul's grandson Christopher.

~~~~~~

Hester Day Roach's story is a mirror of turn-of-the century times told only as one could who had experienced the good and bad times, sometimes back-to-back, but always told with love for her family and a precious sense of humor.

~~~~~~

When Mrs. Roach was interviewed in 1983 she lived in the home she had built in 1939. Now, at 94, she resides in a rest home for ladies but she frequently returns to her home where she relives a past that is gone, but not forgotten. Her sisters preceded her in death.

Seventy-Four Years of Service

The Sisters of Loretto

*Deserving of recognition as women who survived the hardships of life in the Southwest are the Sisters of Loretto who came to Las Cruces, New Mexico Territory on January 7, 1870. They opened their academy and convent and remained in the area until 1944. Information about these women came from a publication printed in 1961, **The First 100 Years** by Rosemary Buchanan. The book tells the story of St. Genevieve's Parish from 1859-1959, and includes interesting historical data about the Sisters.*

On January 7, 1870, five Sisters of Loretto arrived in the sleepy little village of Las Cruces. They were escorted from Santa Fe by Mr. John B. Lamy, a nephew of the famous Archbishop Lamy, and by another gentleman whose name has been lost through the years. It would be safe to assume the men came with them for protection on what was then considered a dangerous journey. Historians believe it took ten days to two weeks to come that distance. The rugged trip included fording the Rio Grande—famous for its quicksand bars—two or three times, and being on the alert for Indians who were still a cruel menace to travelers. It was a rugged trip, but the nuns arrived weary but unharmed.

The five nuns included the Superior, Sister Mary Clara Alarid, Sisters Marianna Dominguez, Jerome Murphy, Gertrude Zamora and Rosanna Dominguez. The Sisters were received by Bishop J.B. Salpointe of Arizona Territory but no convent was ready and waiting for the them. A kindly Mrs. Tully came to the rescue, and took them into her home. There, the Sisters opened and operated their school until their own place could be built.

Loretto Academy on Lohman Street in Las Cruces, New Mexico. (Photo courtesy of Rives Studio Collection - donated by Henry Berroteran. Rio Grande Historical Collections, New Mexico State University Library.)

Sisters of Loretto

Quoting from *The First One Hundred Years*:
> Work on the convent and school was begun at
> once on a tract of land at the foot of Main Street,
> and very soon an adobe structure emerged of
> modest, not to say poor aspect; but as one of
> their historians has said, "Poverty merely chal-
> lenged the zeal of these pioneer nuns." As soon
> as the building was finished they moved in, and
> the Convent of Our Lady of the Visitation was
> filled with the fragrance of prayerful gratitude
> and hope offered by these missionary Sisters of
> Loretto.

Within five years three more sisters joined the little community. They were Sisters Thais Martinez, Agnes Martinez and
Vestina Moran.

Buchanan describes the nun's living conditions in the convent's early years.
> The poverty of the little Las Cruces community
> was evident in the furnishings of the house, even
> in the chapel where the Sisters of Loretto always
> put their very best. Here a rag carpet covered
> the mud floor (which every five days was taken
> up and cleaned and the floor beneath swept and
> sprinkled), the altar was a makeshift board,
> muslin draped, supported on two clothes horses,
> while a small candle box lined with silk and
> covered with green calico served for a tabernacle.
> The rest of the house corresponded...there was
> not a single board floor in the convent.

In 1875, Sister Rosanna was sent as Superior to Taos, and
her place in Las Cruces was filled by Sister Ignatia Mora until
1880. During her term, Sister Ignatia was authorized to estab-
lish a novitiate and had started the erection of a large building.
Mother Praxedes Carty arrived in 1880 as Superior with just
twenty-five cents in her pocket and faced a debt of $5,000.

Mother Praxedes was described as a woman with magnifi-
cent energy who believed in using the abilities God had given
her. Her peers said, "She merely surveyed the scene to deter-
mine where to begin, and then took action."

Mother Praxedes' accomplishments included the building of
a beautiful altar, a Sister's cemetery with white grave markers
and a neat fence. She tore down one of the old adobe

buildings, completed the new building with the addition of another wing, landscaped the grounds; then, as a bit of domesticity in the middle of all the carpentry and brick laying, she presided at the kitchen stove during the canning season. It was said that nobody went hungry that winter.

The railroad came to Las Cruces in 1881. It furnished transportation for the numerous boarding pupils, and, together with the day or local pupils, the school now had a large enrollment. The noviate was closed but the Loretto Academy continued to expand.

In 1880, French Father Lassaigne was assigned to Las Cruces by Bishop Salpointe of Tucson, Arizona. The records show that the second of the little St. Genevieve Churches built in Las Cruces was now shabby and the parishioners had outgrown the old church. The parish had never been wealthy, but as soon as Mother Praxedes had put the "struggling, unfortunate young convent on a firmer basis, she turned her attention to the pressing matter of the inadequate, tumble-down parish church. She and Father Lassaigne went briskly to work to build a new and larger structure."

The First One Hundred Years described Mother Praxedes as an Irish woman with a wheedling tongue in her head and a person who never let grass grow under her feet. Under her supervision the congregation held a church bazaar, the first of its kind ever to be held in the area. It was highly successful. The building fund was augmented by every means possible, including house-to-house collections and various entertainments. The priest and the nun persevered and the money was raised. It was noted that Mother Praxedes apparently appealed to the entire community, not just to Catholics, for the names of other citizens, including the Freudenthals and Reymonds, are mentioned in the archives. The new St. Genevieve's Church was solemnly dedicated in 1887.[1]

Mother Praxedes arranged for the purchase of a statue of the Sacred Heart, and established the League of the Sacred Heart and the Sodality of the Children of Mary. "She advised and mothered the many weary souls who brought their troubles to her."

---

[1] This St. Genevieve's Church was razed in 1967 and replaced by a fourth St. Genevieve's Church built on a different site.

In 1893, Mother Praxedes was transferred to other fields. She rose higher and higher in the Loretto Order until she became Superior General, a post she held through re-elections for twenty years. Mother Rosine Green became her successor.

> ...[She was] a gentle woman with a kind heart. Under her rule the convent prospered. During her administration, in 1897, the Sisters of Loretto began to teach in the Las Cruces public school system. Sister M. Bernard Doyle followed Mother Rosine Green and the convent school enrollment continued to grow. Her successor was Mother Inez Madigan and, during her year, there were evil days—when a terrible smallpox scourge visited Las Cruces and all the convent boarders but one left the city. Had it not been for a lady and her little boy who came to the convent for room and board, the Sisters would have had no income whatever. As it was, their income was only $50 a month.

In the early 1900s, the Loretto Academy expanded. Mother Albertina continued the work of building. Border hostilities in 1916 brought troops to Las Cruces and a Kentucky Brigade marched past the convent. This pleased Mother Barbara, who was from Kentucky. She replaced Mother Albertina and administered the Loretto Academy from 1913 to 1919. During the troubled times of World War I, the nuns and students worked with the Red Cross and Liberty Bond Drives.

The Sisters of Loretto opened the Holy Cross Parochial School at St. Genevieve's in 1925 and a new Loretto Academy was built in El Paso. "...and the poor old Visitation Convent of Las Cruces, which had weathered God only knows what storms and stress, was slowly dying."

Four nuns, Mother Mary Thomas Rodman, Mother Rosine Green—serving a second term, Mother Edmund English and Mother Faber Wheat served from 1919 until 1934, when Mother Barbara returned for another term.

> When Mother Barbara entered her final administration she appeared to have all the time in the world. So far from conducting appropriate funeral exercises over the dear old Academy, Mother Barbara increased the enrollment; and responding to her gentle stimulus the school went

blithely on.

Rosemary Buchanan, the author of *The First One Hundred Years* had fond recollections of a dinner party Sister Barbara gave in the spring of 1934. She wrote:

> Mother Barbara was then confined to her bed with a heart attack, but had planned a dinner and dance for the graduating class, and according to her book the show must go on. The stalwart members of the Newman Club were invited as escorts, the dinner was to take place at a private home belonging to the Misses Mary and Margaret Ronault, and the dance was at the Country Club. It was a beautiful moonlight night in May, with the roses and honeysuckle out in force; and the girls, a dream of young loveliness in their white and blue and pink and pale yellow organdies like a bouquet of spring flowers, were all assembled on the back veranda. They had already showed themselves to Mother who, though on a sick bed, enjoyed and approved of her girls as a real mother should.

It appears in the lives of the good sisters, all was not glum and despair. The beauty of the young women, and the color and festivity of the dance planned by Mother Barbara, were an indication this labor was fulfilling and a joy to the Sisters.

Before the school closed, Mother Bernard Doyle returned for her second term. Mother Louis Marie Kroeger served until 1942, when Sister Cecelia Marie Kaune succeeded her as Superior. She was the last of a long line of dedicated Sisters of Loretto who contributed so much to all phases of education in Las Cruces.

A remembrance of the old Loretto Academy was put up in 1941. The wayside shrine of Our Sorrowful Mother was dedicated as a part of New Mexico's second Cuarto-Centennial Celebration and is still in existence west of the First National Bank Tower on Lohman Avenue.

In 1944, the Franciscan Fathers from El Paso bought the Loretto Academy, and the convent and school were closed. Some of the Sisters stayed in Las Cruces and taught at the Holy Cross School. Others were recalled to the Loretto Academy in El Paso and a number transferred to various locations.

The official historian for the Order of Sisters of Loretto

wrote, "The convent of Las Cruces has joined the ranks of closed houses, but the good accomplished by the Sisters who lived and labored there will go on into eternity."

~~~~~~

This silver medal given to Genevieve Martinez Lucero by the Sisters of Loretto is one of her most precious possessions, reminding her of her youth in the old Loretto Academy. The size of a fifty-cent piece, the medal is dated 1812-1912 and commemorates the Centennial of the Sisters of Loretto.

~~~~~~

ENCLACES CON EL PASADO -

LINKS WITH THE PAST

Sophie Rodriguez Waldrip

Sophie Rodriguez Waldrip generously shared stories about her great-grandmother, her grandmother and her mother when I interviewed her in May 1991. Now eighty-four, Sophie recalled how the women in her family survived floods, droughts, disease, discrimination, Indian raids and family tragedies.

My great-grandfather, Jose Maria Ramirez, was one of the very early settlers in the San Miguel, New Mexico area which, at that time, was part of the Territory of New Mexico. He married my great-grandmother, Doña Inez who was part Indian. I don't think she was a full-blooded Indian but she was of the Apache tribe. They had three children, two girls and a male. I remember that my great-grandmother was small, and dark-skinned, with white hair. In 1920, she died at the age of 106. She never complained about an ache or a pain and never wore eye glasses. The last time I saw her was a day when the sun was shining so pretty and I stopped by to talk to her. She was in the front part of the house sitting by the window in the sunlight mending my great-grand-uncle's socks. My great-grandfather Ramirez, built his house in San Miguel about

Opposite page from top — Doña Inez Ramirez, Margarita 'Lita' Enriquez Moreno, Juliana Moreno Rodriguez, Sophie Rodriguez Waldrip. Women linked by family and religion.

143

1854. All the neighbors came to help, like they did in those days. That is the house I live in now. At first there were earthen floors in the rooms and the women would wet them down. During the time my grandmother lived there they put in the wide wooden floors.

My husband and I renovated the house when we moved into it in 1948. All adobe, the outside walls are twenty-eight inches thick and the inside dividers twenty-four inches thick. You can't hear anybody or any noise from one room to the other. The house is very cool in summer. I hardly ever use the air conditioning we installed. The house has been a haven for some member of the family all these years and now is my home.

I can remember seeing my great-grandmother Inez cooking in the kitchen on a hearth in front of the large fireplace. She would sit on the floor when she was making her tortillas or whatever she was cooking. There was a huge kettle that would pivot on an iron bracket over the fire. The Pilgrims used similar pivoting kettles on the eastern seaboard.

Doña Inez, like all wives in those days, was very submissive. She, as well as the children, did what the head of the family told them to do. I never knew my grandmother on my father's side, Longina Ramirez Moreno. She was dead when I was born.

My mother's mother, was the grandmother I knew. We lived next door to each other. Her name was Margarita Enriguez. Friends and relatives called her Grandma Lita. She married my grandfather, Don Eugenio Moreno, when she was fifteen and he was sixty-five. It was a pre-arranged marriage. My grandfather had been married before and he had two daughters and a son by his first wife. His son, Don Preciliano, was the first pharmacist in Las Cruces. Grandma Margarita and Grandpa Eugenio had ten children.

My grandmother Margarita was very active. I didn't know my grandfather because he was very old when I was a child. What I heard from my mother was that when he got sick as he aged and my grandmother had to take over. She managed the farm and the workmen. My mother, Juliana, who was the oldest, had to take care of my grandfather. He was always in a room by himself. He couldn't get around so my mother took his food to him and cared for him while my grandmother was working outside on the farm. In those days they raised mostly wheat and some corn. In later years the farmers in the valley raised grapes for wine, and grew peaches, apples, cherries, pears, plums and strawberries. They had some irrigation but when the rains came, and they did come, San Miguel would be flooded and the farmers would lose their crops and have nothing to harvest. When it flooded, water come up to the outside of the house.

Life was very serious for the family then. Grandmother was always very busy. In fact, she was a midwife, and when people would call on her to deliver a baby, she would have to make arrangements to have someone take care of the farm while she was gone. She used to deliver babies from near El Paso to Old Mesilla. She was the only licensed midwife in those days, since there were no rural doctors. The nearest doctor was twelve miles away and it took three to four hours by horse and buggy to get to him. All through the valley Grandma was known as La Senora Doctora. She used to say, very proudly, that in all the valley, she never lost a baby or a mother. They would come in a wagon to pick her up. Sometimes she would stay overnight or until the child was delivered. When she went to a home to deliver the baby she would say, "All the children leave the room. I don't want any children around me." So she would send them out. She chased the husband out too. After the baby was born she would come out and tell the children that she had brought a child into the world.

Grandmother Margarita also took care of sick people all over the countryside. She used various kinds of herbs as medicine for pneumonia, colds, and different ailments that people developed. She had chamomile, which was good for many things, Cascara Sagrada, [sacred hide] a laxative and good for digestion, Gordo Lobo [fat wolf] for colds, coughs, and asthma. She was very good at taking care of the different families who were ailing or had some kind of sickness. I wish I had learned more from my grandmother, but I did learn some about herbs from my mother. Interestingly, when you travel in Mexico you can order Chamomile [mansonia] tea anywhere. They always keep it.

Social life at San Miguel in the 1860's up to the early 1900's as I remember hearing about it, centered around my great-grandmother, Inez's, big living room. That's the house where I live now. Whenever the people living in the area had any kind of a meeting, a dance, baptism, or other special occasion, they used that room. They were mostly Catholic families but their small adobe church had no hall. I remember that room had a

Juliana Moreno and Donaciano E. Rodriguez on their wedding day.

mural painted on the back wall. It depicted the life of Christ and the saints. I wonder now why we didn't leave that mural. It was fading away, but we could have had it touched up. San Miguel now has a Catholic Church made of lava rock.

Because she was part Indian, we believe my great-grandmother must have been converted to the Catholic faith. The fiesta and all the community gatherings were always held in my great-grandmother's living room until 1912, when the State of New Mexico became part of the Union. That year the state allowed some funding to build the first public school in San Miguel. After that time, the community used their new three-room white brick school building for their meetings and other events, replacing my grandparent's large living room.

Music was always heard in the village. There were violinists, and guitar and harmonica players ready to perform. When I was older I took piano from a lady from the East who came to San Miguel and also from a professor who came from Mexico. He started a choir for the church and I was the organist for almost thirty years. He taught the girls in the choir to read music. He had an instrument called a harmonium, a little piano that he could fold in two like a suitcase. Wherever he sat down, he would open it up and play it.

My grandmother, Margarita Moreno, was a great storyteller. We children would gather around her out in the patio to hear stories about the wild Southwest, the Indian Geronimo and other folk tales that had been told to her by her parents. When the Apache tribe was in a camp a mile or more west of our village of San Miguel, sometimes they would go on the warpath. The Indians came down from the hills or mesas on food raids. All of the family's livestock and poultry were gathered into the patio and the large entry gate secured. According to family history, the inhabitants would fight and stall the Indians, or bargain to restore peace. The houses were built like fortresses with wooden shutters inside and outside the windows and a high wall surrounding the house. That's why the house was built in an L-shape.

Years later those Apaches were moved onto what is now the Mescalero Indian Reservation.

In addition to all her other work, Grandma Margarita did all the cooking. In those days they did a lot of canning, and drying food and vegetables to keep for the winter months. They preserved enough food for the winter and I guess never went

Margarita 'Grandma Lita' Enriquez Moreno

hungry. They would butcher the pigs and cows and keep the pork in salt water and dry the beef. They used all parts of the animals. Sometimes when they butchered they would invite all the villagers to come in and they would finish the whole thing. My mother was a terrific cook and in her generation they would do the same thing about preserving food as they did in grandmother's time. In those early years they didn't know about cholesterol and used lard for baking and cooking.

My grandfather, Jose Rodriguez, came from Spain as a young man long after the Conquest. The group he came with went different directions from Tampico, a seaport city in Mexico. My grandfather came north to Chihuahua and in 1854 to San Miguel, New Mexico where he was granted land by the King of Spain under the Land Grant Sanchez y Sanchez.

My mother, Juliana Moreno, married my father, Donaciano E. Rodriguez on February 24, 1900 in Old Mesilla, New Mexico. She was nineteen and he was twenty-four. I had three brothers and three sisters but only my brother is now living. The village was a healthy and pleasant community. We grew up playing all the old children's games. The only excitement we had was when a circus from Mexico visited the community, or maybe a magician would come now and then.

One frightening time I remember so well was when Pancho Villa invaded Columbus, New Mexico, south of Deming. General Pershing immediately pursued him with his troops. The excitement lasted for several days and people were careful, fearing that he might hit again closer by.

When I was growing up we didn't have any doctors in the village and many of the infants died at birth or when they were very small. My sister died when she was thirteen years old. She had meningitis and nobody understood what happened to her. She went to school and developed a headache. The teacher took her home to my mother. The whites of her eyes were red and my mother knew she was very sick so she put her to bed. My mother tried to help my sister but she went into a coma later in the evening and died the next morning. That was really a tragic thing in the family. My father called Dr. McBride and Dr. Sexton from Las Cruces to come. They examined her and said it was spinal meningitis. They quarantined the school but no one else got it.

My mother was completely devastated. She just couldn't get over her daughter's death. She thought that it was the end of

her life. For months and months it was so hard to talk to her.
My grandmother used to come in and try to build her up. I had
another sister who died when she was just a child so I was the
surviving daughter and my brother was the only son. I was
sixteen when my sister died.

My mother finally got over it. A missionary priest came to
the village. He used to call her Julianita and he said, "The only
way you can get over this is to adopt a child." She said, "Oh, I
don't think so." My father would say, "If you want to adopt a
child, it's all right. Let's try it." The priest finally convinced her.
This priest was stationed in El Paso and he called mother one
day and told her about this baby that was six weeks old. My
mother and father went to Hotel Dieu in El Paso and they
adopted the little girl. It worked out all right for mother but
now my relationship with my adopted sister isn't what it should
be.

My mother took in boarders—the teachers from our school
—and did sewing to help out my father. She was a very good
seamstress. She was taught how to sew by the nuns when she
went to the Loretto Academy in Las Cruces. She stayed in Las
Cruces with my uncle, who was the pharmacist, and his wife
during the school year. The money she made from sewing
helped my father financially. At that time my father worked on
a farm for fifty cents a day. Mother would sew for people in the
Mesilla Valley and from as far away as El Paso. Then she started sewing for brides and bridesmaids. If the bride showed her a
picture of the bridal gown she wanted, mother could make the
pattern and sew the gown just like the picture. She got well
known and made a name for herself as a seamstress for bridal
gowns. She made enough money so we could have things that
we couldn't have afforded with just what my father earned. My
mother would buy us kids toys. We had a room where we kept
the dolls and we had all the furniture for the dolls—the living
room, kitchen, dining room and the bedroom. My sister and I
used to spend a lot of time playing with the dolls in that room.
This was when we were quite young, before my sister died.

Something else my mother used to do, that was an important
part of my growing up, was going to El Paso to concerts. Most
of the performers and musicians that we saw in the theater
were from Spain. The plays were in Spanish.

Waldrip

In many families there are near tragedies that seem so terrible. After it is all over, the humor of the incident is evident. Sophie Waldrip related this story about her mother, which turned out to be funny but could have had another ending.

At the outbreak of and during the First World War there was an influenza epidemic. The village of San Miguel was devastated by it. People were dying every day. My mother was the only one in our family who didn't get it so she nursed everyone of us. She had my brother in one room, my sister and I in another room, my father in another and the house help in another. My uncle, Preciliano Moreno, who was the pharmacist, sent her medicine to give us. But Mother felt that we were not getting better fast enough. After several days she decided to give us a hot toddy one night. It was during prohibition days but my father managed to buy regular whiskey, as well as a pure alcohol for medicinal purposes. So my mother gave us a hot toddy that night. The next morning none of us woke up at eight, or nine or even ten in the morning. Mother thought we were all dead! She checked to see if we were breathing and we were so she left us alone. She became very worried but waited patiently but wondered why we couldn't wake up. She decided to check what she had given us and went to the closet where the liquor was kept. She found out that instead of whiskey she had made the toddy with pure alcohol! She didn't know what the results would be or what to do, so being a religious woman she prayed. We woke up that afternoon with no fever and feeling fresh. Mother checked every one of us. She embraced and kissed us and said, "Thank God, you have come back to me." She told us what she had done and began to laugh. Poor mother, she was so tired and worn out because she was unable to rest or sleep all those days but she was able to joke about what happened. Afterward, she enjoyed telling the story.

Sophie's great respect for her father and admiration for how her mother encouraged and helped her father are very touching. Her love for both parents weaves through her life like a golden thread.

All the grandparents in my family spoke Spanish. My mother learned to speak English when she went to the Loretto Academy but my father, Donaciano, didn't speak English until he married my mother. My father's father, Jose Rodriguez, didn't think my father needed to be educated or speak English. He said, "With the farm that you have you don't need any schooling." In those days the people in the community used to contract with a tutor from Chihuahua to come to San Miguel for three or four months and he would teach the people who were interested how to read and write in Spanish. My father was very interested in learning English. When my mother was boarding the teacher who taught in the San Miguel school, the teacher would teach my father English in return for her meals. Of course, being bilingual my mother helped him with his English too. My father became quite fluent in both languages and was an eloquent speaker. Without my mother's influence, faith, and moral and physical support, the dreams of my father, D. E. Rodriguez, the humble farm boy, may never have been realized.

I remember how it was when we went to Las Cruces to shop or get tools for the farm or garden. My mother would awaken us early in the morning. Father would take out the one-seated buggy, harness the horse and at seven in the morning mother and we kids would leave for Las Cruces. We would arrive around noon. Mother would park the buggy at the north end of Main Street where you would find a public water trough for horses. She would unharness the horse and tie it close to the trough for hay and water. Then she would take us to Uncle Precy's pharmacy and we would wait for her there until she finished her errands. Uncle Precy had a waiting room in his drugstore for the people. Mother then fed us at an old-fashioned country dining room. At about two o'clock we would begin our trip back home, arriving in the evening tired and happy.

The Rio Grande was always a threat and at that time was considered very dangerous. I recall one time when the Rio Grande overflowed its banks for a distance of three miles. Flood waters covered the land and the fields that were about to be harvested so the farmers lost their crops again. These floods happened so often, that many men in the community owned their own row boats so they would have a way to cross when the river was high.

One time my Aunt Mary was visiting Uncle Precy's family in Las Cruces. When she was returning the bridge went down under and the team of horses kept churning away for the shore. All I could see of my aunt was her big straw hat floating in the river. They finally made it. The horses were used to this adventure and knew what to do as well as the driver.

My grandmother and my mother always helped with the church. The first church was a small adobe structure and the parishioners decided they would start raising funds for a new church. One way they did this was every month my Grandma Lita and my mother would get the ladies together and they would have an enchilada supper. The enchilada plate would sell for twenty-five cents. You can imagine how long it took them. Then they would have a dance and charge twenty-five or fifty cents for the dance. People would gather and come from the surrounding area and camp out.

They used to have box suppers too. My grandmother used to tell the girls to fix their box so their fiance would know it and he would bid on it. Many girls would put something in the box for a surprise and when the man opened it something unexpected would happen, like a jack-in-the-box, would pop out. It seemed like the fund-raising went on for centuries, but finally they had enough money to build the church. That's the church that burned two or three years ago and now is rebuilt.

My mother told me that Grandmother Margarita delivered me. I grew up in that fourteen-room house. My mother had someone to help her with the housework.

Another story from my childhood was about the big St. Bernard dog that my parents taught to take care of me. My mother used to say when I was crawling, I would crawl outside on the porch. The house had a more-or-less lobby entrance. I would go almost to the outside of the house and the St. Bernard would pick me up by the neck and bring me back to the inside of the house.

I do remember when I was in school and Ruth Hyland was my teacher. I don't know what I did wrong, but the teacher picked me up, put me on her lap and spanked me with her hand. I yelled and yelled and I jumped up, left the room and went home crying. You would think somebody was killing me. When my mother saw me she said, "What's wrong with you?" I said, "Mrs. Hyland beat me!" Mother said, "What did you do?" I said, "I didn't do anything." Well, she thought we should go talk to the teacher so we went back to school and they gave me another spanking! You think I did that again? No, I did not! If I was ever disciplined in school again, I never told my mother.

After I graduated from the eighth grade in San Miguel, I went to Las Cruces High School. I boarded with a family my father knew. In the 1920's, when my father was elected Sheriff of Dona Ana County, the family had to move to Las Cruces. My last years in high school I lived at home.

I also took music lessons at the Loretto Academy and Sister Dolores taught me art. I still do a lot of art work—china painting, water colors and oils. I keep busy now doing crafts. It was the Sisters at the Academy who insisted that I coax my parents to send me to college. That is why I went to Webster College in St. Louis, Missouri. It

Sophie Rodriguez Waldrip leaving San Miguel School on a windy day.

was a college run by the Sisters of Loretto. I went for two years and then the Depression came and I had to come home because my brother was ready to go to college and with the Depression my father couldn't afford to keep us both in college away from home. I came home and got my degree here at New Mexico A & M, and my brother went to school at Austin, Texas.

Sophie's education came full cycle when she returned to teach at the school she had attended as a child. She recalled what a professor had told her in college and how she applied it when she taught at San Miguel.

My professor had told me it was not wise to teach in a community where you were born because it is not logical and you may not be successful. That was his idea, but I considered it and for me it was a challenge. I always feel if there is a challenge, I work on it. I went to my own community and I was a successful teacher, due to the fact that I was aware of what he told me. He thought one wouldn't get respect, but I did get the respect. I stayed there quite a while teaching until I went back to the university to get my master's degree.

When I went to elementary school in San Miguel we were taught in English. Years later I came back and taught in that same school. I had sixty students and I worked very hard teaching them English and at the end of the school year they could speak it and ask questions. They had done beautifully. In fact, for what I accomplished there, I was given a scholarship to the University of New Mexico.

In 1931 I became State Supervisor of Education in charge of seventeen one-room schools and four high schools scattered all over Sandoval County. Three of the high schools were taught by the Sisters of Loretto, the Franciscan Sisters, and the Christian Brothers. They were all public schools. The Sisters and Brothers owned the buildings and the state rented them. The schools were public, but the teachers were from the three orders.

I had an old Plymouth car I used to drive when I visited the schools. I remember one time I had to leave my car and get a horse to get to a school. The school was near a small river. I have kept a picture of each of those schools. There were two schools that were way out in the country. I felt so sorry for those teachers. They worked so hard. In order to warm one of the school rooms a fellow gave a teacher one of those large tin barrels. The teacher managed to fit it with an opening to put the wood in just like a heater. Some of the other teachers did the same thing. Think about the teachers nowadays. They just wouldn't do it. I was so proud of those women. I managed to visit every school on schedule. They would tell me about their students and I would admire the teachers because they would go out of their way to help the children. They were pioneers in education. It seems the children accomplished much more too. However, when things got too political with the state I resigned from that position.

I met my first husband when I was state supervisor. I had two daughters, Jackie and Irene, but that marriage didn't work out. He just wouldn't stay in one job, and why say more. The marriage didn't survive and I got a divorce. My family didn't believe in divorce but I had to do it that way.

That's when I came home and started teaching in the Lower Valley. When a position opened up in Gadsden High School I began teaching there and that's where I taught for twenty-six years.

I met my second husband [William Waldrip] at the University of New Mexico. He was from Indiana and was working on his master's degree in education, too. He was out of the Army after World War II. He had been stationed at different bases in New Mexico during the war and decided to come back here after he was discharged because he liked this part of the country. We were married in Albuquerque and he came to Doña Ana County and got a job as principal. We had a beautiful life together. We traveled a great deal. We went to Mexico, all over the United States, to Europe including Ireland, and to North Africa. On our last trip to Europe in August 1960, when we were in Paris, he had a slight heart attack. Before starting the school year, he had to take a physical examination. The doctor said his heart was damaged a little. He didn't take care of himself. He didn't quit smoking and he was supposed to stay home for at least six weeks, resting and reading all he wanted to. After I left the house he would go and play basketball with the children. He didn't do what the doctor told him. That's what killed him. He passed away on December 5, 1968, and I was left alone again. I've been by myself ever since.

My daughter, Jackie, lives in the house that I inherited from my father and teaches at Gadsden High School. My other daughter, Irene, lives in Albuquerque and is an auditor for the Army. I have five grandchildren and three great-grandchildren. I am very proud of my family.

Thinking back on what I had to overcome during my life, I think about the time I went back to Gadsden High School to teach. I took the place of Christina Amador who resigned. I saw the ad in the newspaper for the vacancy, but the last day for applying was on a Monday and it was Sunday. It was the job I had been hoping for, but I thought it was too late. My father said, "It's never too late." I talked to the man who was principal. He knew me when I went to school at Gadsden. He said to call the school board members, which I did, and I got the job as Spanish teacher.

When I started teaching there a group of Anglo boys made the remark, which I heard afterwards. "We had a Spanish [Hispanic] teacher here but we aren't going to have another one." I said to myself, "They are not going to force me out." I had the backing of the board, the principal and some of the teachers. The boys were sons of Klu Klux Klan members. When my father was sheriff he checked the influence of the Klan, which had established itself in the county. The organization lost its effectiveness, which resulted in ending the group's activities and the threat to the people of Doña Ana County for a time. However, my father lost the election and the next sheriff was sympathetic to the Klan, so Klu Klux Klan activities started again. Controlling those young Klu Klux Klan boys in school was another challenge for me.

When I was supervising the study hall one of the group of Anglo KKK boys started harassing me. The other boys joined in. They threw paper spitballs, messed around with books and made all kinds of awful noises. I told them to stop it. They said, "You make me!" They did everything—made noise with hairpins on the chairs. It was horrible. Finally one of the leaders said, "You can't make me." I told him to leave and he wouldn't go. One of the older teachers from across the hall came to the study hall and stood in the door. She told them all to get out and they went out of the building and after that things got better. That was the stormy beginning of my twenty-six years of teaching at Gadsden. I retired in 1966.

Teaching was my life and still is. I have my students come in all the time. They stop by and see me. Others are scattered all over the world—in California, Boston, Africa, and one who was in Arabia and married a princess there. She died and now he is married to a dancer and lives in Santa Monica. Some of the students and I got together in Guadalajara a few years ago and had a good time. For me, teaching was very rewarding. I don't think it is that rewarding now. I am happy because I have all my students coming to see me. They build me up.

In 1965, when my father was losing his eyesight, he couldn't do what he had done for the Democratic Party for so many years. I took over as the Democratic Party Precinct Chairperson in the village. I did follow in his footsteps. I was candidate to the state convention and vice-chairman of the Democratic Party. Later on I ran for County Clerk. I was defeated by a young girl who campaigned saying that I didn't need the job.

That was discrimination. People who knew me thought there was no possibility of my losing and they didn't go vote. So I lost. I have been active in the party until recently when it became hard for me to get around because of arthritis.

My father's political career, which began when he was nineteen, is another interesting story. He "broke the ice" for the Democratic Party after years of the Republican Party's reign. He was the first Democratic sheriff for the county and held other important federal and state offices.

I was always eager to help the elderly and it was very satisfying to be able to be one of the pioneers in working, expanding and directing the Munson Senior Citizens' Center in Las Cruces. I was with the Munson Center from 1974 until 1980, and helped draw up the plans for the present building.

~~~~~~

Sophie Rodriguez Waldrip has received many awards and honors throughout the years. She received the 1975 New Mexico State University International Woman of the Year Award for her work as Director of the Munson Senior Citizens' Center. In 1978 she received The Southwest Community Woman of Achievement Award from the Association of Women Students of New Mexico State University. She has chaired the State American Association of University Women's state meeting, the Pan American Round Table Convention and presided and held numerous offices in educational and community organizations including the Democratic Party.

~~~~~~

INDEX